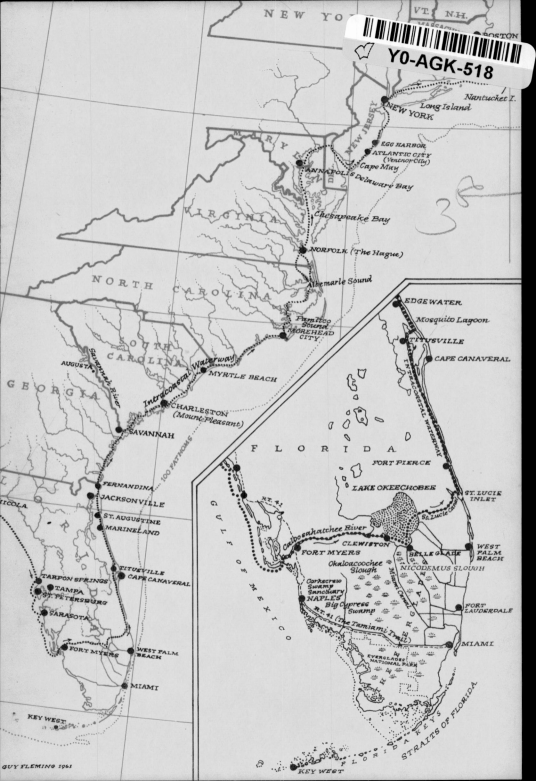

BOOKS BY JAN DE HARTOG

PLAYS

WATERS OF THE NEW WORLD

JAN DE HARTOG

WATERS OF THE NEW WORLD

HOUSTON TO NANTUCKET

DRAWINGS BY JO SPIER

ATHENEUM : NEW YORK
1961

TO THE MEMORY OF

Bob Wickman

DEAR FRIEND

Portions of this book have appeared in
Harper's and The American Scholar

Library of Congress catalog card number 61–13559
Published simultaneously in Canada by Longmans, Green & Company
Manufactured in the United States of America by
Kingsport Press, Inc., Kingsport, Tennessee
Designed by Harry Ford
First Edition

PREFACE

To many Americans it must seem that no foreigner able to wield a pen can visit the United States without writing down his impressions. For some reason, these always turn out to be condescending; there must be something about America that compels the visitor from abroad to measure himself against it, the way David measured himself against Goliath. Speaking for the foreigners, all I can say is that the puny visitor with his little suitcase, assailed by the question "How do you like America?" within minutes of his arrival, soon feels like a frog fleeing from a steamroller, to end up on his hind-legs, beating his chest, crying, "I hate you!" before he either leaps back into the pond from whence he came, or is turned into part of the road.

When I arrived in the United States, my situation seemed different. Instead of arriving with just a suitcase, I brought my house along: an old seagoing barge that had been my home for years and on which I now set out to travel about the New World. In a way, I stayed in Holland: when I drew the curtains at night, I might as well be moored to the bank of a Dutch canal. Instead of fleeing from the steamroller, I drifted along on a water-lily leaf: a calm, dispassionate frog, who felt not compelled to condemn but inspired to serenade, oblivious of the circumstance that, though frogs are called "Dutch Nightingales" in Holland, they might be called something different somewhere else.

Yet I did not altogether escape the visiting alien's

reaction. My first impressions, as recorded in this book, are those of a wayfarer who has not yet discovered that man's journeys, when all is said and done, are meanderings down a gallery of mirrors. I felt that America was a hostile giant, an enemy of frogs.

There is a Chinese proverb "Do not pursue your enemy; sit down on the river's bank and wait for his body to float by." In the stillness of the bayous on the Gulf of Mexico, the solitude of the Florida lakes, the silver expanse of the Sounds on the Atlantic seaboard, I came to realize the wisdom of that adage. The point of it, I discovered, was not that the enemy's body would eventually drift by; it was simply a device to halt the panting warrior, make him drop his weapon and sit down. Once he had done so, and started to look at the water, the reeds, the sky and the clouds, he was bound to be touched by the dawning realization of his own evanescence in the timeless pageant of nature. He would start musing about life, love, death, immortality, and forget about his enemy.

This is what happened to me. As I sat watching the river, musing, I realized that what I had started to write were not impressions of America, but sketches for a self-portrait. I had used the waters of the New World the way Narcissus, more modestly, had used a pond. So there is no justification for calling this volume a travel book on the Inland Waterways of the United States of America, which I set out to write, or a collection of essays on Modern Man in Nature, as I hoped it might turn out. All it is, is a book of songs by a Dutch Nightingale to the moon rising over the land of man's new hope.

J DE H   *Ship Rival*   1958–1961

CONTENTS

1 *Texas*

CONTENTS

THE SHIP

LIKE many Hollanders, I have lived most of my adolescent life on the inland waters of the Old World, and most of my adult life at sea. After the war, following an abortive attempt to settle ashore, I bought my own ship.

Rival was an old, venerable sailboat of 146 tons, 90 feet long and 16 feet wide, very Dutch in appearance with leeboards and rounded bows and poop, reminiscent of the galleons of yore. She had been a coaster for forty years, sailed as far south as Casablanca, as far north as the head of the Baltic and as far west—one hazardous trip— as St. Johns, Newfoundland. She left Holland with cheese and came back with lumber; when I bought her the smell of cheese was still evident in her small, respectable holds.

Rival belonged to her captain, who had sailed on her ever since he was an earnest young man. She was built in 1908 by an adventurer who wanted a fast ship and who, after her maiden-voyage, nearly beached her in fury because she wouldn't do more than five knots in half a gale. He offered her to his deck hand for an insulting price; he was, so the deck hand told me forty years later, trying to insult the ship by robbing himself.

The young deck hand took him up on the offer, bought her with a mortgage, and sailed her slowly and cautiously to the Baltic, with his young bride for a crew. Forty years later he said, "Rival turned out to be a calm, gentle ship, kind to the man who treated her with respect." The adventurer had a new ship built, a rakish schooner that matched him in both temperament and speed; they vanished together on her second voyage, without a trace.

The young man sailed on with his calm, gentle ship, taking turns at the helm with his wife; their eyes and those of their baby turned bluer as, year after year, they gazed at the sea and the sky. When he talked to me of those early years, a lifetime later, gazing out of the small windows in the poop of his ship at the seagulls and the oily water and the flotsam of the ships' cemetery where she lay dying, those young summer days of hope and joy seemed only yesterday. He did not want Rival to rot and die just because she was his and he could no longer sail her; she was not his, she was, like all of us, no one's property but the Lord's.

So I took her over from him and converted her into a sailing houseboat and put in an auxiliary engine; when I took her out to sea and she gently rose and fell with the swell of the open, I knew that the old man had told me the truth when he said that she was calm and gentle, and kind to the man who treated her with respect. We set out on long voyages together: through Belgium and France to the Mediterranean; back to Holland up the Rhone and down the Meuse; I sailed her as a hospital ship during the flood that destroyed one fifth of our country in February 1953. She was all I had hoped for; despite her fifty years and her ponderous slowness she seemed, at crucial moments, suddenly young and lithe,

and made me feel the same. Kindness was indeed her
outstanding virtue.

Occasionally, in wintertime, as she lay at anchor in
the fog of the delta of the Rhine, or moored at a quay
in the Seine, I indulged in a daydream: to take her across
the ocean to North America, and explore with her the
waters of the New World. She was too old by now to
make the crossing herself and would have to be shipped
to the Gulf Coast on the deck of a freighter, but she was
ideally suited for the shallow rivers and creeks of Louisiana and the lakes of central Florida, and she was still
sturdy enough to make the outside passages of the Atlantic seaboard on calm days.

One night, moored near an old lock in Holland, I
tentatively outlined a route. From Houston, Texas, via
the Texas Intracoastal Waterway and the bayous of
Louisiana to New Orleans. From there along the coast
of Mississippi, Alabama and northwest Florida to Apalachicola; then across the open Gulf to Tarpon Springs,
Clearwater, St. Petersburg and Fort Myers. From that
southernmost frontier town across the Florida jungle by
way of the Caloosahatchee River and Lake Okeechobee,
right through the heart of the mysterious Everglades.
Then up the East Coast, through the water-wilderness of
Georgia and the Carolinas, to Chesapeake Bay, the Po-
tomac River, Washington, Annapolis; and, finally, down
Delaware Bay and through the creeks and lagoons of
New Jersey, to New York. That was quite a voyage,
but my fancy took me further. Up the Hudson River to
Lake Champlain, into Canada and to Montreal; from
there up the St. Lawrence to Lake Ontario, Lake Erie,
Lake Huron, Lake Michigan, Chicago; from Chicago by
Illinois Waterway to St. Louis on the Mississippi. Down
the Mississippi and back to New Orleans? As I was just
doodling on paper, and as the crackling of the logs in

the fireplace and the warbling of the canary and the small excited yelps of the ship's dog dreaming in front of the fireplace made the very image of security, I rounded the wide river bend in St. Louis and swung up the Missouri. It would take me, despite current, rapids, banks and bogs, all the way across the great Midwest, through Missouri and Kansas, Iowa and Nebraska, the Dakotas and Montana, to the brink of the Far West: the Fort Peck Reservoir, and Fort Benton in the foothills below the Continental Divide. It seemed a wonderful way of seeing the New World: years at the wheel of an old, slow ship. Years . . .

Then the dog woke up from his dreams of youth in front of the fire, and looked round at me, and lifted his tail in a drowsy wag of sympathy. I realized that I had been doing the same as he: running through the fields of youth with winged feet and a heart as light as a flying cloud, to wake up in front of the same flames that had bewitched my simple, drowsy friend.

I laid down my pencil and concluded that it had been a nice but useless way to spend an evening.

THE GREAT DANES

THE FOLLOWING morning I stood in front of the mirror, razor poised, and heard outside the familiar sounds of home awakening. The lock-keeper's chickens cackled as the old man opened the gate of their coop for their morning feed; the neighboring farmer's dog barked at the freight train as it whistled at the level crossing; a blue jay laughed maliciously as it swooped down on Mrs. Petersen's tomcat, dragging his neutral languor to the ash patch. I listened to these sounds, so familiar and secure, and thought I must have been mad to think of having this ship, my very home, pulled out of the water like a radish and carted off across the ocean to the other side of the globe, to be let down among the alligators and the coral snakes of Texas. I shrugged my shoulders, and shaved; this Aladdin, for one, would never rub his lamp.

All explorers, victims of man's insatiable curiosity, must have been overcome by this hesitation. Why must they fall victim to their feeling of unrest, that dark, pulsating urge to open the last closed door? The old legend of man in Eden: all doors are open, except one, and it is in front of this one closed door that Adam sits, brooding, his back turned on the cackling chickens, the laughing jay and Mrs. Petersen's tomcat, now prowling his private jungle of two dandelions, a nettle and a three-week-old oak tree. I sighed and rinsed my razor, and summer went by. I remained tied up at the dock. It was a good place to work. Rival slept.

One morning in the heart of the next winter, when the flooded fields of the delta lay waiting for the frost that was late that year, I heard shouts on the dock. I looked out of a porthole and saw the lock-keeper standing in the flat, low light of the winter, excitedly waving his arms and crying, "Look! Look up there! There go the Great Danes!"

I thought he had gone mad, and tried to peer up at the sky through the porthole; I saw nothing but the stave of the telephone lines that followed the dike, dotted with sparse chords of sparrows huddling together from the cold.

The lock-keeper went on pointing at the sky and shouting, and I came out on deck. As I looked up, blinded by the wintry sun, I heard overhead an angry, high sound, a regal bickering, and saw a flight of white swans circling down toward the flooded field. The lock-keeper explained, his words puffs in the frosty air, that they were swans from Denmark, and that it meant we were in for a severe winter. Had I ever seen such a magnificent sight?

The Great Danes planed down for a landing in temporary confusion, but they did not touch the water. Something in this small corner of the mighty delta of the Rhine, with its mud flats, reeds, disused duckblinds and two little men standing on a dock must have disappointed them. They swooped up again, took up formation and winged away.

I stood staring at them as they vanished, silver in the sunlight, toward the far horizon of their longing. Then I turned round and went down the dock, past the lock-keeper's chickens, the farmer's barking dog and Mrs. Petersen's cat toward the telephone booth on the other side of the lock. As I stood waiting for the operator to make the long-distance connection with the shipping company, I saw, far away, across the fields, the white plume of the freight train as it whistled for the level crossing.

I never discovered why the Great Danes took off again, nor why I went after them, on that particular morning.

THE LOST CAP

THERE are images out of stories one reads as a boy that one never forgets. I must have been about fourteen when I got out of the school library a book called *The Dutch Boy's Book of the Sea* which contained naval stories for the young that were highly unsuitable. One described the last moments of a sailor who fell overboard while painting, upside down, the lettering on his ship's bow. He saw the vessel pass over him and I remember to this day the very words that evoked the image: "As he gazed upward, there passed over his head a dark, whalelike shadow, the last he was ever to see: his ship."

When I stood gazing up at the dark, whalelike shadow of my ship, silhouetted against the January sky, I felt uncomfortable indeed. There she hung, between the sea and the clouds, suspended from a gigantic crane like a caught fish; and there was the angler, peering down at his catch from a glass penthouse in the armpit of his monster. We looked at one another, the crane driver and I, and despite the distance between us something in my gaze made him grin comfortingly and wave that most homely of objects: a half-eaten bun. I would advise the pilot of any air liner in danger to pass down the aisle, a half-eaten bun in his hand, and all his passengers will

go to sleep with a sigh of relief. I heaved a sigh of relief,
and to show the crane driver my trust, I pointed my
movie camera at him. It was a reckless thing to do; he
at once stuffed the bun in his mouth and started to
operate levers with a natural talent for the drama, send-
ing the one hundred and forty-six tons that dangled at
the end of his line soaring through the sky toward the
vast expanse of new timber laid out on the freighter's
deck that virile experts had referred to as "a cradle." I
went on filming while the sky darkened and had to be
pulled away as my ship was in the act of sitting down on
me. At last she was down, calmly, and sedately; the crane
driver had surpassed himself. I climbed on board and saw
that not a chair had moved, the canary was warbling in
his cage. The ship Rival was now stacked on top of the
ship Witmarsum, and together they sailed out of
Antwerp harbor, their Dutch flags flying in the westerly
breeze.

Many a time I had visualized this very departure; yet,
now it was here, it seemed completely unreal: the old
barge on the deck of the new freighter, the lock with its
customs officers worrying how to list these two ships,
and beyond that the vast gray Scheldt with its untidy
flock of barges swinging into the current to anchor for
customs at the Lilo gas buoy. I had passed customs there
myself a month before, when sailing to Antwerp, and I
had admired the nonchalance with which the colossal
barges swung in unison, five abreast, with Belgian housewives polishing portholes, Dutch housewives stringing
up laundry lines and French housewives polishing their
nails. Now these same barges looked small, seen from
the windy bridge of the freighter, and I heard the captain
say to the pilot, "I wish they would move the check
point for that small fry a mile or so upstream—they are
forever running between our legs down here." I smiled

down benevolently at the small fry, the five-hundred-and three-hundred-tonners that had dwarfed Rival as she swung with them into the current a month before; and, as if some sprite of the inland waters were outraged, my peaked cap which had served me for many years and arrived at that state of shapelessness which made it irreplaceable, was blown off my head and vanished, a bird's dropping, in the turbulent eddies of the river Scheldt.

I was to sail to America bareheaded, balding in the wintry sun, until I could buy a ten-gallon hat and be inconspicuous once more among my brother Texans.

THE CROSSING

THE SMALL group of passengers in the dining
saloon of the Dutch freighter on its way across the
Atlantic might have been found on board a windjammer
a hundred years ago. There was the young couple on
their way to the New World, the husband smoking a
cigar that looked slightly older than himself, the pregnant young wife earnestly embroidering baby's bibs
with chickens and rabbits which could not possibly
mean anything to a baby. There was the didactic, slightly
pompous young engineering student, gazing over the
heads of the diners at a private vision; there was the
elderly couple intent on manners, with the synchronized
movements of their heads which a long, happy marriage
seems to bring about. And on the other side of the table,
the hardy perennials: the salty old captain, gold-en-
crusted, breathing fumes of good cheer across the table
and assuring everybody that after the Azores the

weather would be much better; the placid Chief Engi-
neer who had taken the place of the doctor a century
before and who represented materialism by smiling
knowingly at everything; the First Officer, the only one
in that dining room who ever did a stroke of work and
who sat there, after hurriedly changing into his uncomfortable best, frowning at his soup as he worried about
the shifting deckload, cook's emotional illness and the
mislaid bill of lading of that grand piano for Corpus
Christi.

Yet there was a difference, and that was the ship. In
the days of the windjammer, the sounds of shrouds and
straining sails, the creaking of the ceiling must have
receded into the background after a day or two at sea; on
board this modern vessel the St. Vitus's dance of the
internal-combustion engine contorted every mealtime
into a gathering of patients with delirium tremens. The
cups rattled on their saucers, the pictures clattered on
the walls, the ship's dog lay panting under the table as
the tremors of Doctor Diesel's disease brought him to
the brink of a fit. The fear of the elements of a hundred
years ago, which was the fear of God in disguise, had
been replaced by the fear of man's self-created monsters;
the slaying of the dragon of the doldrums had been paid
for with the triumph of the demon of vibration.

The only place where I could escape the constant and
unrelenting trembling of the ship and everything and
everybody inside it was on board my own Rival, which
sat sedately on the deck. The moment I entered her old-
fashioned cabin, fed the canary, watered the plants and
went about a bargee's business, quietly pottering for an
hour or so, I felt liberated from the neurotic world of
the trembling freighter.

One morning, as I filled the minute drinking vessel
which the canary stubbornly used as a bath, I suddenly

became aware of the personality of the old ship. For a strange, disembodied moment, she was no longer a steel barge blindly going where I wanted her to go, but a person waking up to a magic reality. Here she was, after fifty years, on her way to an adventure that thousands of her proud contemporaries had never dared to dream of. She had never been a beautiful or a remarkable ship; her lines were plain, her bow was homely, the sweep of her deck too prudent and the cut of her stern too stiff. I had bought her because she happened to be the last sea-*tjalk* that was still afloat; the others of her vintage had been transformed into coal barges, or lighters, or floats for the square superstructures of immobile houseboats. And now, during this eerie voyage to the New World, on the back of this freighter racing across the wintry ocean with the arrogance of youth, she seemed to wake up to the miracle that had been bestowed upon her. The bos'n of the freighter, who came from a family of Dutch bargees and was born on a *tjalk* like her, was the first human being in fifty years to look at her through narrowed eyes, like a painter, and say: "That's a lovely vessel, you know."

I gazed out of the small windows in her poop, as her first man had done so often during the past fifty years. There was nothing as far as the eye could reach but the gray waste of the sea. As I stood there, the tiny bird bath in my hand, I shared her awakening to the reality of her graceful hull, the sweep of her deckhouse, the power of her bows, the soaring spire of her mast. I saw her on the bayous of Louisiana, on the Gulf of Mexico, on Lake Okeechobee—romantic white sailboat from a faraway shore—and I knew that she would be beautiful to behold, and that I would be proud to sail her, and that the great voyage ahead of us would be triumphant and glorious, a new song to Him Whose property we were.

TEXAS

THE UNLOADING of Rival from the freighter's deck in Houston was done by two floating cranes, and the procedure was very different from what it had been in Antwerp. Delighted Negroes in highly colored shirts swarmed over her deck, sat down at the huge wheel, turned it, pulled the fore-and-aft handle, blew her hooter and squealed with laughter. A stevedore in a mushroom-colored desert outfit tried to organize them into a crew; he stood on Rival's roof, conducting the drivers of both cranes with a symphonic waving of his hands. The old ship left the deck and jerkily started her journey through space, with both cranes blowing clouds of steam and the Negroes waving and cheering. In Antwerp every living soul had been ordered off her before she had started majestically to rise from the waters; in Houston she looked like the boat of a merry-go-round, all gilt and scrolls, swarming with cheering children. Her rudder hit one of the cranes, which resulted in an allegro furioso from the conductor's hands, then her bows hit the other, at which he shook his fist in the direction of the wood-winds. During all this, her flag fluttered gaily, the setting sun beat gold out of the oily river and the whole world seemed to be waving flags as the colorful shirts of

Texas weaved in and out of the sunlight and the shadows, now lengthening in the coming dusk.

I felt elated. Here she was, in the New World; this was the beginning of our great journey. Yet I am sure I would have felt the same elation had I arrived as a traveler with nothing but a kit bag and a hat. There was, in the air, a vitality and a hope that brought back memories of French, English and German harbors in the twenties, the ports of my youth.

When Rival finally sat in the water, and her holds had been checked for leaks and her engine tried out, we were ready to sail away into the night under our own power. It had been arranged that she should be taken to a small boatyard nearby, where she was to remain for a couple of weeks to be fitted out for the trip. The owner of the boatyard was on board to pilot her there, a lanky, smiling Baptist in khakis, given to girlish shrugs and coy hand-wavings that would have looked incongruous on anyone else. After waiting patiently, wreathed in smiles, for a moth's lifetime, he was ready to pilot us down the Ship Channel and up a narrow winding creek called Brays Bayou. He had warned me that there were some hairpin bends to negotiate, and that here and there there might be an obstruction in the shape of a bridge or a sunken craft, but apart from these it was plain sailing.

It was a balmy, romantic night, with a full moon floating in the haze behind the mast-tops of the freighters lining the channel's bank. We sailed back toward the sea, nosing our way cautiously among the barges and the tugboats; it was marvelous to be transported in one swoop from Antwerp's icy Yuletide to this midsummer night. Our pilot told me that the creek where his boatyard lay was going to be widened to seventy feet and turned into a boatman's paradise; but, for the time being . . .

For the time being, Brays Bayou was a tricky patch of water indeed. Submerged piles, wrecks across the channel, unlighted boats moored right up to the other bank and not a beacon or a buoy anywhere, let alone a light. There was one low bridge across a main thorough-fare called Broadway where we had to moor, waiting for the operator. He arrived some twenty minutes later in his own car, and told us that we had to wait another twenty minutes for a policeman: after nightfall, the bridge could not be opened without an officer to regulate the road traffic. We waited and, in due course, a police car with screaming siren and flashing red light drew up at the bridge, tires squealing. A police officer got out, called a cheerful "Hi!" down to the waiting ship, lit a torch that blazed bright magenta and billowed smoke; bells started ringing, red lights flashing; an engine raced underneath the bridge and it slowly rose, carrying policeman and operator aloft, waving their torches and blowing whistles. It was the kind of operation that would have delighted a five-year-old or an ancient Indonesian sultan; Rival sailed proudly under the bridge and the pilot cried out: "Watch out! There's a sunken craft over in that corner!"

It was yet another one in a succession of sunken craft, and while we crawled up the pitch-dark bayou, the pilot told me the story of each one of them, stories from Mark Twain and Melville. Cicadas chirruped in the shrubs on the banks; but for the pungent stench of fuel oil and gasoline, this might have been a century ago.

The little boatyard was timeless. Ever since man started to mess around in boats in the Dark Ages, there must have been places like this on the banks of the rivers of the earth: a few small craft asleep in the moonlight, a dark shed among the trees, a black crane among the stars and a boy on the jetty calling, "Here, Mr. Pete!

Ah'm here!" We moored in total darkness; the ropes
were secured ashore by a bodiless voice calling, "Here,
Mr. Pete! Ah'm here!"

Then the engine fell silent. The crickets crowded into
the breach; and here was Texas.

THE PIRATE SHIP

I HAVE never climbed a mountain, but I know how a climber must feel when, approaching the summit, he is faced by a sheer wall of overhanging rock. That's how I felt when, after all this time, effort and expense, my ship lay finally moored in Brays Bayou off the Houston Ship Channel, ready to cruise through the United States.

She was not quite ready to sail, but could have been considered so at a pinch; the sheer wall of overhanging rock made me decide to put her in shape before setting out. There was a lot to do, once I decided to set out with a ship looking like a yacht; I could easily spend half a year working on her in the oily waters of the bayou, amid the stench of refineries, the racket of highway, level crossing, boatyard and foundry.

My worst night was the second after my arrival in Texas. There were the cicadas, but they fought a losing battle with the ungodly racket man made underneath that glorious starry sky. Ambulances screamed across the bridge, followed by the hyena howl of the undertaker's hearse; the double Diesel engine of the sugar train stood clanging its double bell for minutes on end at the level crossing and at the same time a tugboat passed, blaring, through the tunnel of the lifted bridge, on top of which the alarm bells rang in the night at a pitch of spiraling lunacy. It was possible that a certain branch of the human species might feel at home here; I did not belong to it. Never in my life had I felt so alien to my surroundings; God only knew what had possessed me to take myself and my ship halfway round the globe to put ourselves here, in Brays Bayou, Houston, Texas.

The next morning seemed to bring some relief, but it was short-lived. I asked the charming people of the boat-yard what they would charge for giving the ship a coat of paint if I provided the materials; they went into a huddle and came out, radiant, with an amount that, in Europe, would have had her metalized. Then the ship's dog came back, looking sheepish, and smelling, of all things, of cheap perfume. The old bos'n whom I had brought across the ocean with me to be my gay and sparkling companion throughout the trip of six thousand miles stated that he had a toothache, didn't like America and wanted to go home. In view of the fact that I wanted to go home myself, I suppose I was unduly harsh with him; the atmosphere that descended on the ship was one of unutterable gloom.

As I sat on the aft deck, head in hands, I heard a rustle on the shore, and whispers, but I refused to look up. I was not interested in anything except in the answer to the one great question, "Why?" Then someone ashore secretively called, "Psst!"

I looked up, and saw, peering at me from the bushes at the water's edge, three little boys and a dog. They were a Negro, a Mexican and a little white boy with freckles to whom the dog obviously belonged as it was attached to him by a piece of string. They were clad in blue jeans and T shirts and the little Mexican wore cowboy boots. The white boy opened his mouth to speak, but the Negro put out a warning hand and peered up and down the dirty ditch, that slowly changed into a tropical river under his anxious gaze. The shrubs seemed to change into an eerie jungle of tangled trees; the raucous singing of a welder inside the echo chamber of an iron hull on the shore suddenly sounded full of malice. The Negro boy nearly lost his balance, as he leaned forward, cupped his hands and whispered, "Is this a pirate ship?"

There was a silence in which even the dog looked at me with reverent expectancy, as I peered up and down the river myself. Then I put my finger to my lips and said, "Ssh!"

I was an alien no longer.

A DENTIST

So THE bos'n had toothache, and it was a Sunday.
His teeth, when I inspected them with a mixture of
horror and awe as he breathed an old "Ah" into my flar-
ing nostrils, looked like an archaeologist's find, and
seemed beyond redemption. "I don't want any black-
smith monkeying with them," he said belligerently,
glowering at the shore as if there stood a crowd of hairy
men in overalls armed with wrenches, "I want a dentist
like Mr. Kubbenga, who did my uppers. He was an
artist."

I set out on a quest for the artistic Mr. Kubbenga's
opposite number in Houston, Texas, on a Sunday morning, with a feeling of futility. My bos'n growled and
groaned in the background as I dialed a number, one
finger in the yellow pages of the telephone guide under
the heading, DENTAL SURGEONS.

In the end, I found a person willing to plumb my
bos'n's cavities on the Sabbath. He told me briskly to
turn up at the Medical Center in half an hour's time with
the patient, thirteenth floor, corridor E, office number
1369.

A taxi took us to the Medical Center, a blue and pearl-
gray rectangular edifice; its ground floor was taken up
with various shops that go with the trade: a pharmacy, a
flower shop, a baby mart and a mortician. As I stood

paying the taxi driver, my back to the entrance, I heard music. My bos'n leered at the dark hall and asked, "What's the band for?" I said I didn't know but that I supposed it came from a cafeteria round the corner. It did not; as we entered the hall we found the music came from loudspeakers in the ceiling; they nasally hummed, "Hello, young lovers, wherever you are," while we waited for the elevator. The bos'n looked around with suspicion. "I knew a dentist," he said, "who always turned the radio on loud before pulling." I said, "Fancy," then the elevator doors slid open of their own accord. The bos'n followed me inside; when he heard music coming from the ceiling of the elevator as well, he frowned. The doors silently slid shut behind us; we were whisked up with sinking stomachs to the thirteenth floor; the doors opened, and we faced a dimly lit corridor, also filled with soft, hypnotic strains of music.

A big man stood waiting for us at the far end and called, "This way, folks." We joined him, in a cubistic waiting room, and found him to be a muscular giant of Slavic complexion who, to my bos'n's alarm, rolled up his sleeves as he looked him over and said, "All right, choose. Do you want the blue or the pink room?" We were shown two identical chambers with padded seat, searchlight and dangling chromium equipment, one decorated in pink and the other in sky-blue. From both oozed the melting ice cream of "Nature Boy." My bos'n was ushered into the pink room as he could not make up his mind; the dentist said to me, "Take a look at the magazines. We won't be a moment." I sat down in a sighing chair, picked up *Look* magazine, opened it at random, read Dr. Norman Vincent Peale's advice to a young minister's wife whose husband was turning ascetic (take him to a psychiatrist); and then, suddenly, the music became louder.

The dentist came out first. As I rose reverently to my feet, he said, "He'll be round in a minute, but really what you should do is to have the lot out. It's a graveyard."

I thanked him for his advice, and then my bos'n appeared. He reeled to the door, staggered to the elevator, and weaved out of the building to the strains of "Catch A Falling Star."

As we sat, finally, in a taxi on our way back to the ship, he said: "No difference. They are all the same." He wound down the window, spat at America, and concluded: "Everything is the same."

He went home soon after.

A VISIT TO FOLEY'S

THE AMERICAN department store is a unique in-
stitution, and Foley's in Houston is more than American,
it is Texan. I went there to buy blue jeans; the moment I
entered the ice-cold Aladdin's cave from the broiling hot
street, I felt as if I were intruding upon a private party.
Not that the crowd inside was alien toward me, but
they were pursuing a goal that I could not discern. All
of them looked like caricatures of the Texan as drawn by
clever New York cartoonists; even little girls, chattering
birdlike on the electric escalator, wore tiny three-gallon
hats, and when I arrived on the second floor I was struck
by the incredible spectacle of a colossal woman dressed
in white sharkskin, adorned with tassels, spurred boots
and a white ten-gallon hat, with, under her jacket, the
reversed bulges of two pistols.

It must be said that it was during the week of the Fat
Stock show and that all the salesmen wore black string
ties with, in gold lettering, GO TEXAN, while the cars outside carried notices in their rear windows saying, BUILT
IN TEXAS BY TEXANS. So perhaps the crowd in Foley's was

more aggressively Texan than usual, yet there was something impressive about the earnestness with which they had put on the accoutrements of the cowboy. When I came to the blue jeans counter, I was initiated into the lore of the plains by a small cowhand with a Hungarian accent. He was about five feet tall, with applelike buttocks and prim hips, and pirouetted in front of the full-length mirror, scrutinizing the fit of the jeans he was trying on. "Ah," he said. "These are no goot. You see ze fold in ze back underneath ze belt, just over ze tailbone? Dat is a sign they are not ze real ones. But then, you see, zese are pre-shrunk, that's why. Buy a pair that will shrink, buy 'em one size too large and let zem dry on your body."

I said I would.

"Been here long?" the little cowboy asked.

I said I had arrived the previous day.

"You will soon feel at home," he said, "if you follow my advice. Buy a hat."

I asked him how long he had been here.

He answered, quite sincerely, "Ach, a lifetime."

The salesman, who called me "pardner," looked at me with a critical eye and said he only had my size preshrunk.

"Don't fall for it," my little friend cried. "If you buy zose, it'll take you months to become a Texan!"

I bought a pair of shorts.

THE AZALEA TRAIL—1

A COUNTRYMAN of mine who had married into Texas offered to show me some gardens on what was called "The Azalea Trail." This was a thing every lover of beauty must see: the ornamental gardens of the "permanent families" of Houston.

I looked forward to the outing with some apprehension. A howling norther was blowing after an icy night; the blue suit my host had suggested for the occasion was too thin and my overcoat too thick. When he emerged in tweeds from a station wagon and greeted me with a sporty handshake, my apprehension deepened to gloom.

As we drove through the perpetual outskirts that are Houston, he told me about the first garden we were to visit. It belonged to the famous Old Lady of Houston, Miss Ima Hogg, whose father had had a virile sense of humor. It was totally untrue though, so he said, that her sister's name was Ura. This was typical of the exaggeration with which Yankees would describe anything Texan.

When we arrived at the gate to Miss Ima Hogg's garden, there was not an azalea in sight, as they had all dropped dead overnight and been swept away by the norther. The house at the far end of the graveled drive looked gray and sad in its genteel decay. It was the kind of house in which aristocratic spinsters used to live in Europe, before the war. There had been one near my parents' home in Holland, just as gray, and the lonely old lady inside had been called "Miss Gloria."

My guide stopped the swept-winged station wagon in front of the porch, turned off the radio, got out and rang the bell. A colored butler in lilac livery opened the door, and when he was asked whether Miss Ima was at home he answered with respectful condescension that indeed Miss Ima was not. So we saw only the gardens. There were old trees standing patriotically about on an immaculate lawn; there were marble Grecian statues bending over ponds and there was somewhere, behind the old cobwebs of the Spanish moss, a dovecot from which bird-large butterflies winged up into the dark foliage. We strolled toward a statue that I could not place in mythology, but that looked like Leda waiting for the next swan; as we walked around her, I spotted underneath her marble seat a little red tin with bright lettering: an anti-snake-bite kit.

My host said it was a pity I couldn't see the azaleas, because here I was truly facing the true Old South. The true Old South stared at me with infinite sadness from heavy-lidded windows with looped and tasseled curtains across the immaculate lawns, where the old male trees stood on guard over the old lady who had taken a life-time to give the lie to her name. As we went past a side door on our way back to the car, there was a high yapping in marble halls; through a crack peered a dark face at eye level and a little snout at ankle level. "Yes," my host said, "everyone has miniature dachshunds nowadays. They are an adorable breed." As we drove back the few hundred yards to our century, I turned round and caught a last glimpse of the old gray house through the rhododendrons. It seemed to me at that moment that the true Old South was a small boy's world as remembered by any middle-aged man. My Old South had been Miss Gloria, and as the car swept out of the gate, I sent a lighthearted little prayer winging toward her, a butterfly from our dovecot earth in search of her gallant soul among the suns, the stars and the planets, azaleas in God's garden.

THE AZALEA TRAIL—II

"Now," my host said, "I'd like to take you to a slightly more modern home, more compact, with some lovely tropical shrubs in the garden. You'll find it very restrained, for so rich a man."

We stopped in front of a concrete house, defiant in its pink stark-nakedness among the ivy-clad French châteaux and vine-veiled English manor houses of Millionaires' Row. In order to reach the garden, we had to cross a cocktail party indoors.

The first to welcome us was a twelve-year-old girl with a miniature dachshund in her arms, halfway down a flight of stairs, both of them looking delightful. There is something about children, who should be in bed, hovering on the brink of a party, that is irresistible.

The adults were gathered in a garden room, a strained, noisy lot armed with wide bourbon glasses wrapped in individual napkins so as not to chill the hand. The men looked tired and the women tense, and everybody was laughing with that openmouthed laugh which tries to force the rest of the face to join in the fun.

Yet they were charming. Even before the colored

butler in blue livery had brought me a tomato juice, I had been invited to spend a month in the woods up north this summer with my whole family, never mind where I was at the time, because my newly won friend would send his private plane down to pick us up. "Now come and meet Arthur. He's in the insurance business, and he's a scream." Arthur was much bigger than I, which made me react to him with the characteristics of a small man: I looked up at him with admiration and hated his guts. There was also a portly gentleman from Chicago who told a funny story about a mix-up in hotel rooms during a convention, and there was Grandfather whom I must absolutely meet because he knew everything about the Erie Canal. Oh, the garden! Of course! Let's get out there, quick, before it is too dark to see.

The garden was a paved sidewalk around a blue-tiled swimming pool, bordered by bamboo and plants with big rubbery leaves that, in my horticultural ignorance, I lumped together as gum trees. The most interesting thing in the garden was the pool because, so our shivering hostess explained as we stood in the norther, it was heated. Look, up there were the thermometers, one for the air which stood at forty-eight, and one for the water which stood at seventy-three. Her husband swam every day and once he was in, it was real hard to get him out. Well, it sure was nice to have met you, Mr. Warthog, and do hurry back and see us. As I passed him, Arthur slipped me a card which said, *Work is the ruin of the drinking classes.* We were drummed out into the hall by the rolling thunder of his laughter. And there was the child; still halfway down the stairs, holding the little dog tight against her in an unconscious effort to communicate her delight to someone alive. "Isn't it a wonderful party?" she asked, in a whisper.

"Wonderful," I whispered back, ignoring the pleading

look of the puppy, suspended between earth and sky in mute resignation. Ah, if only I could start the azalea trail all over again, from the point where she now stood, gazing down upon the glittering glory of the adult world!

But then we stood outside, in the gathering dusk and in the icy wind that came from the great plains of the Lone Star State. "Let's hurry," said my host, "before we catch our death."

I hurried, resolutely, determined to enjoy life, all of it, before Death caught me.

THE AZALEA TRAIL—III

BACK in the station wagon, my host said, "Now the next lady, I must warn you, is a bit churchy. Lost a son in the war, you know, that kind of thing. But a really lovely garden. Very old family, you'll see. Collects pottery too."

The doorbell of the dark, tidy house was a long time answering. At first it seemed as if there were nobody in except a dog with a high-pitched bark which sounded like another dachshund. Then a boy's voice asked from inside, "Who is there?" and my host told him it was his uncle, with a very nice gentleman who had come all the way from Holland just to have one little peek at that lovely garden of Granny's with all those beautiful . . .

She opened the door herself, and I had met her many times. She could be English, Dutch or German, because to her War had no nationality. There was something about her that suddenly illuminated the dark, elderly house and turned it into the kind of house young lieutenants dreamed about in the trenches of Flanders or

Korea, never to see again. The dark hall felt as if there were tennis rackets and baseball bats about, and long woolen scarves untidily thrown on the umbrella stand; but it was all in the atmosphere. She introduced the young boy to us, rather nervously, as David Somebody the Third. We said, "Hello, David," and the boy looked at us with intelligent curiosity through steel-rimmed glasses, and showed his braces in a grin. "They're all wrap up," he said. "Granny has put pots and boxes over all the flowers because of the frost." "Oh yes," she said. "Dear me, there really isn't much to see," but presently we stood in the garden, which was small and neat and lined with newspapers and upturned cardboard boxes. David the Third called in the background, "You see? They're all wrap up," and she said, "Go along, David. Go and finish your meal, there's a dear. I'll be right back. Now here," she said, "is a little plaque I put in after I sat here one evening in the rain." Her hand rubbed aside the leaves that covered a bronze plaque with a quotation from the Bible about rain, the Shepherd and peace. "There's another one," she said, "over there in that corner. I—I'm so sorry about the flowers, about there not being any, I mean. Here it is." It was another quotation about pastures, and protection, and peace.

We saw some more shrubs and upturned pots and peeked at something white through a tear she cautiously made in a newspaper; then we suddenly stood in a small enclosure where there was a little fountain and a marble cupid and another plaque with a quotation. "This was a corner my son liked very much," she said, "so we turned it into a little garden of remembrance. He died in 1944." She did not mention the war; all she had mentioned when she stooped to read out the quotations, like a searching mother stooping on a battlefield, was peace.

As we crossed the lawn in the failing light, my host

stumbled over a roller skate left on the path; when he picked it up we saw it was a toy tank.

"Hurry back now!" a gay boy's voice called after us from the shadows of the house, as we closed the gate.

THE WRECK OF
THE MARY LOU

ACROSS the bayou, at a stone's throw from the little boatyard where I was moored, lay a half-submerged wreck on its side. The wheelhouse was still partly out of the water and bore the marks of high tides; across the dark cavern of its hatchless engine room lay the bough of a willow tree, trailing in the water.

There was about the old wreck an atmosphere of sadness, for even from her pitiful remnants it could still be seen that she must once have been an old sailor's pride. The handrail on her flaked roof was carefully painted in a different color from the little stanchions, and her name, Mary Lou, in manuscript, looked as if it had been traced by a hand that was sternly ordered not to tremble. The people at the boatyard told me that she had belonged to an old sea captain who had lived on her for years until he died without leaving any next of kin. Now the wreck was just waiting for the Army Corps of

Engineers to blow her up when they widened the bayou next year. All she was now was a sagging, empty shell; the name of the man who had loved her was remembered only by his ghost.

But one morning, as I sat looking across the water at the old wreck, I discovered that she was full of life. The first I saw emerge from one of the windows of the wheelhouse was a turtle, who looked up and down the stream before venturing into the open. Then it paddled along the sunken foredeck toward the splintered stump of the bowsprit and cautiously hoisted itself onto it, to bask in the sun. Then there appeared, on the roof, the secretive silhouette of a big tomcat, who also peered cautiously around before slithering down the slope of the wheelhouse roof and disappearing gymnastically inside. The appearance of the tomcat caused an unexpected movement in the gray handrail of the engine-room stairs that led down into the black interior, and I realized that what I had taken to be the handrail was the neck of a blue heron. Its very presence betrayed that there must be a secret activity in the engine room of flitting fish and water-treading frogs, and indeed, as I listened carefully, I heard above the rattling of the steam hammers, the clanging of the railway bells and the racket of the traffic in the distance, the bragging croak of an extrovert frog. The tomcat's passage caused yet another commotion: along the sloping ridge of the gunwale flitted the fleet shadow of what must have been a scurrying rat. A children's storybook slowly turned its delightful pages as I sat watching from across the bayou, and then its hero appeared.

He was a little Negro boy, followed by a mongrel on very short legs. He emerged from the deserted village that had been evacuated by the Corps of Engineers for the widening of the bayou and climbed down the steep

bank of the river. He did not look up and down the river
as the animal crew of the Mary Lou had done, but lowered himself straight into the wheelhouse, the little mongrel under his arm. Once inside, he pulled a lever, talked
through the speaking tube to the engine room, sounded
a silent hooter, took the wheel and slowly turned its
broken spokes.

As I sat watching the boy with mounting envy, I
heard in the engine room the sudden splash of the heron's
patience rewarded, saw the turtle dive into the bayou for
its afternoon dip, and it seemed as if, on the willow's
trailing bough, there sat the ghost of an old sailor, laughing and rubbing his hands.

AN INVITATION

HE HAD come strolling by and stopped to watch me several nights running before he spoke: a squat little man with a serious expression, who looked very clean in the untidy boatyard where I sat picking the rust off the anchors and silvering them until it became too dark to see. The evening sky stood green behind the angular silhouettes of a half-finished barge, the crane and the shack, and the frogs started to roll their dice in the mangroves across the bayou where the deserted Negro village lay.

On the night he spoke to me, he had his wife with him, as short and stocky as he, but smiling the secret smile of imminent surprise.

"Nice boat you've got there," he said.

I had now been in America long enough to know how to reply to a compliment. I said, "Thank you."

"You from over there?" he asked.

I said, "Yes."

Then he nudged his wife and whispered, "Go on, say it."

His wife swallowed, a little nervously, then smiled and said, "Ernuh bernuh nernuh urn." At least, that's what it sounded like.

I said, "Pardon?"

The man frowned. "No understand?" he asked, and whispered, "Say it again."

His wife, one foot in front of the other, repeated slowly, full of meaning, "Ernuh bernuh nernuh urn."

"I'm sorry," I said.

"How come you can't understand that?" the little man inquired suspiciously. "I thought you said you were from over there."

"I am."

"Well, so is she. She invited you to dinner, in Danish."

"Ah, I see. I am Dutch."

"Oh, well," the little man said with an impatient gesture, "what's the difference? Anyhow, are you coming?"

"I beg your pardon?"

He came very close to me, took his hands out of his pockets and said quietly, "She invited you to dinner. She is from your country. She'll make you a barbecue that'll take your breath away."

I said, "Ah, I see. Well, that's wonderful. . . . The only trouble is, I'm sorry about this, but I'm a vegetarian."

"Well, that's fine," the little man said. "She's cooked for vegetarians hundreds of times. She'll broil you a goat."

"Yes, but you see, I don't eat goat. I mean—a vegetarian doesn't eat meat—I mean . . ."

"I know, I know," the little man said, his impatient gesture more aggressive, "but this goat is different. You see, the way she does it, she injects the sauce into the animal before it is cooked. Boy, after a meal like that, you won't know whether you're home or abroad." Then he turned to his wife. "Now say it again," he ordered, his hands dangling ominously.

The little woman swallowed again and looked at me pleadingly as she said, "Ernuh bernuh nernuh urn."

I said, in Dutch, "Thank you very much. That is very kind of you."

"What did he say?" the little man inquired.

The little woman answered, "He said he would love to come some time next week."

The little man grunted, "Good. Be seeing you," and they strolled away into the darkening dusk, arm in arm.

A YOUNG TEXAN

If the swamps of the Texas jungle bordering the
Gulf are a virgin wilderness waiting for its first man,
then Texas itself is a virgin nation waiting for its first
poet. There are moments when, strolling along the busy
streets or letting yourself be carried along by the jostling
crowd, or just standing and watching a young craftsman
working with solemn concentration, you feel rising
from them the surging melody, wordless as yet, of a
great song of brotherhood. There they are, blown across
the globe by all four winds, nesting together in the arid
plains, the hostile swamps; and the ten-gallon hats,
high-heeled riding boots and tight jeans which look
ridiculous at first on a Polish taxi driver or a German
doctor soon reveal themselves as attempts to set up sym-
bols of a new nation.

Texas is a new country, and as I stood watching the
lanky boy who mended the ironwork on my ship's mast,
I listened to him idly talking with his mind on his work
and saw behind the silhouette of his bent head, stooped
shoulders and narrow pelvis the dawning profile of a
nation.

He talked about his father who had been a carpenter, about the hot sun of summer on the dust bowl of the plains, about the junior high where the flies buzzed against the windowpanes while the sweating teacher droned on, about his first car which had been a Model T, the best car in the world, and his first girl friend, who had been rather fat and was sure to be married by now to a realtor or an insurance broker because she wanted to get on in life rather than to go for rides in a Model T with a thin carpenter's apprentice, to stop on the treeless banks of the round lake where the meteor had struck and listen to the frogs hollering in a landscape as barren as the moon. Then he lowered his dark goggles and lit the welding torch and cut the iron with a shower of sparks; and as he stood waiting for the dark red glow to cool off he talked about the fiddlers that came with the cowboys and the songs they sang, full of names, like Johnny Luger, son of William, whose mother was the daughter of Red Flensburg and the Cherokee squaw; and the men and the girls would dance in the sand until their shoes got too hot, and then they would kick them off and dance on barefoot while the fiddlers got wilder and started to yodel, and when the heat and the drink and the tunes and the dancing had whisked everyone into a frenzy of screams and yodels, the thin young boys, without girls as yet, would turn cart wheels of elation against the starry sky, and they would wake up the coyotes who would yodel back from the great plains, and in the end it would seem as if the very stars, the biggest in the world, the real Texas stars, joined in the shouting. When I asked him what the shouting had been about, he scratched his head behind the goggles in his hair and answered, "I sure wish I knoo."

The day he knows will be the birthday of a nation.

THE LAST HORSE IN TEXAS

As I drove round Galveston Bay in the car I had hired, I came, in the midst of a forest of derricks that had spilled over into the very bay, upon a sign decorated with flags saying, GET YOURSELF A LITTLE PAL! JOHNNY'S PET SHOP HAS EVERYTHING! ALL SPECIES FOR ALL AGES! HURRY! The last word seemed to be the only tribute Johnny had paid to the modern times that had now engulfed him. I turned off the metalized road onto a much-worn track, and drove cautiously past the nodding pumps, the creaking derricks, the telephone wires humming eerily in the wind.

Johnny's Pet Shop turned out to be a small bungalow with a lean-to filled with empty cages, and surrounded by small flower beds, or at least I assumed that was what they had been. Right now, they looked as if a herd of hogs had rooted there. A gaunt man came out of the porch when he saw the car bounce onto his property. He asked me what I wanted and when I said I had come to have a look at his pets, he answered, "They're gone, friend. Everything's gone. Ah cain't stick it here any longer. Ah'm going to open a new business somewhere else where there ain't no oil, and ah'm taking MacCrory with me." I assumed that MacCrory was his partner, but when he realized from my conversation that this was the case, he said, "Hell, no, he ain't no man. That's him, over there, and if you ask me he's the last horse in Texas."

I looked in the direction of his gnarled finger, stretched out toward the sunset, and there I saw, silhouetted against the flaming sky, tired and tragic among the der-

ricks, an old horse standing on three legs, its head hanging down, like Rosinante after its noble rider had attacked the windmills and fallen unconscious to the ground. Now it stood there patiently waiting for Don Quixote to come to his senses, but as I listened to the old man the chance of that seemed small. He was going to find a place on the Gulf that was not spoilt, and where there were plenty of horses. He would get interesting animals from all over the place and train them until they were safe with kids. He could make any animal safe with kids, even a tiger; they had respect for the small and the defenseless, wild animals had, but them oil barons . . . "Help yourself, friend," he said. "If you like cactuses, go ahead and dig some up. They are the only things I can't take with me, and I'll be damned if I'm going to see them drown in a pool of petroleum."

I dug out as many cacti as I could spread out on newspapers on the back seat of the car, confident that I would find friends in Houston willing to put them in their patios. The old man stood talking over me as I dug. Darkness fell, and his silhouette among the derricks became as gaunt and quixotic as MacCrory's. MacCrory himself had vanished in the encroaching shadows of the night.

"Yeah," the old man said, as the evening star began to twinkle over his shoulder. "This ain't no place for man any more as God created him in His garden."

For one fleeting moment, my eternal longing for Paradise lost went with an old man on an old horse, trotting arthritically down a Texas highway; then he said, "Well, be seeing yuh. Ah'd better go and give the old boy a drink."

A pump squeaked in the darkness, and there was heard in the oil field of Baytown the last sound of the pioneers: a bucket clanking in the night.

THE BOAT FROM CYPREMORT

I HAD noticed him quite soon after we moored at the small boatyard, off the Houston Ship Channel. I had noticed him and winced.

He was that irritating type of aggressive salesman who, even during his hours of leisure, seems to be beating his fists against the bars of an invisible cage and shouting hoarsely for company. He told me, within the hour, all about himself and his wife, mainly about his wife. She didn't understand him, she was a bitch and he was going to buy a boat to get away from her.

He tried out several boats during the next week or so and you could not help but notice him trying. He roared past in high-powered outboards and cabin cruisers; then, one night, after he had tried a dozen, he confided to me and the trees and the scurrying squirrels that he would be damned if he was going to have himself swindled; the prices they asked for those damn boats would be too high even for a Cadillac, so he was going to buy a secondhand one in Cypremort. I said I thought that was a splendid idea.

We did not see him for over a week, and very restful it was. Then, one late afternoon, there came nosing up the channel the oldest, ungainliest little shrimp boat I

had ever seen. She must have been at least forty years
old, had broad, flat haunches, a perpendicular bow, a
top-heavy fantail and, on her deck, an angular wheelhouse like a privy from which glowered our high-pressured friend, unshaven and snarling. He moored clumsily, and as we helped him with the ropes he cursed the
ship in no uncertain terms. He had been at the wheel for
fifty hours, all the way from Cypremort, he had lost his
way at least ten times and found himself on uncharted
shallow lakes at dead of night, and all this while crawling
along at a snail's pace because the engine would not
come up to sufficient revolutions. He was tired but un-
tiring, and we all felt without saying as much that it was
a crying shame he should have laid his hands on so venerable an elderly boat.

And then, during the weeks that followed, something
happened that first made us think we were seeing things,
then made us frown in wonder, and finally made us
watch with incredulous fascination. The old boat from
Cypremort slowly changed our high-pressured neurotic
into a quiet, concentrated potterer who exchanged his
blazer and white ducks for dirty overalls, his peaked cap
for a sock and his cigarettes for a pipe that went out
without his noticing it for hours. He started by stripping
the old paint off her wheelhouse and giving it a new coat,
then he vanished inside to tinker with her engine and re-
arrange the interior, but mainly to crawl on his belly
through her smelly little hold and lie there, chin on
hands, seeing visions of how he was going to transform
her, without an inkling that it was she who was trans-
forming him.

He took weeks, laboring halfway through the night to
put her in habitable shape, and by the end of those weeks
he had been invited to drop in for a cup of coffee by
various crews that before had shunned him like the

plague. Nobody knew quite what it was that had changed him; whether some old gnome of the sea was hiding on board that old boat and did its eerie work, or whether it was just the fact that the age of his vessel made him feel young. In any case, after a couple of months, he took his wife out in her and although they went very slowly, he no longer seemed to mind.

THE TWO PORTS OF HOUSTON

As ANY Houstonian will testify, the port of Houston is nothing short of a miracle. The Ship Channel which leads from Galveston Bay to the heart of the town was dug when there was hardly a Houston worth speaking of; the town that sprouted round its port like palms in an oasis was the outcome of the daring vision of a few great men. So the traveler who slowly sails up the Houston Ship Channel, churned into constant motion by the never-ending traffic of tugs, freighters and tankers, feels that this man-made harbor is typical of Texas and of the men who made it the richest state in the Union. Of course, he reflects with dispassionate envy, they were lucky, as the whole of Texas has been lucky; the lone star in its flag may well be a tribute to the lucky one. He feels that Texas is the outcome of a great bonanza, and starts explaining its glaring aspects on that basis until, unwittingly, he stumbles upon the truth.

A silent monument to the truth about Texas is the second port of Houston, which branches off the Ship Channel at Morgan's Point. It is an enormous empty basin with depths ranging from twenty to thirty feet, man-made like the Ship Channel and surrounded, not by a hustling town, but by marshes where mosquitoes breed, a few dilapidated shacks long since deserted, and the remnants of old jetties turned into wrecks. This port of Houston was dug by another great man with a daring vision before the city existed, but his vision, sadly enough, was false. For some reason, inexplicable though everyone will try to explain it reasonably, the Goddess of Fortune in her Argo sailed past the spacious basin, its new jetties, its easy entrance, its excellent location, and bestowed her gifts upon the old bayou in the heart of the swamps.

The story does not tell what happened to the visionary who saw his dream sail past and vanish, but the atmosphere of the forgotten port is haunting. At night, when its still waters reflect the stars and the eternally wakeful flame of a distant refinery, all the sprites and elfins that the stench of the oil-rich bayou has chased away seem to congregate in its shadows. The night heron wings silently across the moon's quivering trail, the frogs boast brainlessly in the reeds, a courageous rat sets out into the darkness, trailing a widening arrow of silver. The shores, so tangled and depressing by day with the heaps of refuse and the clouds of mosquitoes, become the meeting ground of a thousand animal voices, croaking, chirping, quacking, warbling, ululating in the transparent darkness, while in the distance, on the banks of the Ship Channel, the bells, the sirens, the loudspeakers, the foghorns, the whistles and the combustion engines of progress hoot, snort, whine and howl.

I don't know where he is now, but wherever he may be, I want to reassure the visionary whom the star-spangled goddess of plenty passed by. Instead of digging Houston harbor, he dug Walden Pond; and there are some who would think him the winner of America's greatest prize.

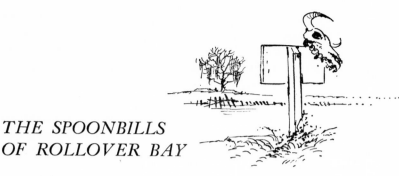

THE SPOONBILLS
OF ROLLOVER BAY

THE MARINER who sets out for the first time on the Texas Intracoastal Canal will be surprised, for this dead-straight ditch has nothing to do with anything else on this planet. It might look familiar to a man from Mars, if the straight dark lines crisscrossing that planet's rusty expanse are indeed canals.

The Texas Intracoastal is obviously man-made, yet it already seems, a few decades after its construction, as if an ancient and forgotten tribe had executed this stupendous work. On either side of the straight and narrow ditch there is the endless prairie, and an eerie desolation hangs over it, like an invisible mist in the still air. There are cattle in the prairie, but they are uncared for and wild; the banks are dotted with carcasses of cows and steers killed by lightning or snake bite; somewhere a lonesome joker has put a horned skull on top of a notice saying, DO NOT DRAG YOUR ANCHOR—NATURAL GAS PIPE-LINE CROSSING.

There are many of these notices along the banks, and the thought of these invisible veins, pulsating with the lifeblood of a civilization, crossing the prairie skin-deep, gives you the feeling, after a while, that you are crawling across the triangle on America's back that, as the Romans noted, is the one region of a man's person that he can never set eyes on himself.

There are no bridges between Port Bolivar and High Island, a distance of twenty-five miles, but there is a short break in the canal's geometrical hallucination as it crosses a small sea inlet called Rollover Bay. A string of buoys marks the channel along a string of small islands; on those islands nest roseate spoonbills and white herons that look from afar like an orchestra of angels tuning up their instruments for a celestial *aubade*. They are not disturbed by passing craft; they strut and flutter, strum and squeak; occasionally they rise a few feet in the air with a stange sound of laughter amidst a small turbulence of seagulls like wind-blown pages of music. The roseate spoonbills of Rollover Bay bring home the futility of man's triumph over the prairie in a lighthearted fashion. His arrival in this vastness is so recent, his departure so imminent, compared to the angels still tuning up after he has left. All the birds on this lonely stretch are obviously feeling the opposite of what the sailor feels as he slowly drifts by. No loneliness here, but a frenzied social activity of coming and going, nipping in, flitting out and flashing across the water. The air is crisp with aviary gossip; every bush, every shrub is twittering with excitement. There are scarlet tanagers, redwings like drum majorettes with red epaulettes; there are the ever-present grackles, the most garrulous birds of the continent, and there are the pirates suspended between land and sky, the broad-winged hawks. So, in a way, Rollover Bay comes as a relief; but by the time the traveler has crossed it, he is happy to be back in the man-made canal and to blow his horn once more, a trumpeting ant in the desert.

There, at last, are High Island's bridges round the bend. There are the reservoirs, bright with silver paint, the derricks, the nodding oil pumps; yet they seem impermanent, flimsy and somehow rather silly. The bridge-

keeper sits in a little cubicle on the second bridge, the
railway one, which is usually left open. He shouted at
me, "Where're you from, Cap? Where're you goin'?"
I called back, "From Amsterdam to New York," and he
waved and called "Okay!" Under normal circumstances,
you would have said, my information might have caused
a pause for thought. Not so in the Texas prairie. I might
have called, "From Erewhon to the Moon!" and he
would have waved and called back, "Okay!" For there
sits a man overcome with pride and joy at the sheer fact
of sitting there, triumphant centurion on the frontier of
nothing, beset by the gay spoonbills, the gossipping
grackles, and forever watched by the silent souls floating unblinkingly overhead.

Then the corner is turned, the bridges, the tanks and
the derricks recede around the bend, and there is the
canal again, twenty-five dead-straight miles of it, as far
as the eye can reach, and there is the prairie on the left
as far as the eye can reach, and there are the marshes on
the right, and there is the sky and the sailing clouds of
the third day of Creation.

THE CHANGING OF THE GUARD

SOME humans do live in the lonely marshes south of the Texas Intracoastal; the lock-keeper of North Prong Locks, for instance, whose little basin I had picked out on the chart as a possible mooring for the night. The word "dolphins" was printed next to three little dots in eternity, and we had been sailing toward them for hours when they finally emerged from the sea-green marsh. But I did not stop as I had planned, for the atmosphere of the little dwelling was frightening: a gray stone hut on the crown of a narrow dike, its windows barred and steel-shuttered, its door armor-plated. I never knew whether there was anybody inside that pillbox, and perhaps that was the idea; but I had the eerie feeling of being watched by the triangular stare of a lonely man and his gun.

The sun was setting, the shadows lengthening; the broad-winged hawk hovering overhead seemed to get broader-winged and blacker. The keeper of North Prong Locks turned out to have been the sentinel of a nightmarish country, for the birds fell silent, the wind died down and the prairie began to whisper. There was still that narrow dike with the path on top leading no-where, but the countryside began to exude terror in-stead of just desolation. It could not be the failing light, yet perhaps it was just that. Some other power was taking over; what we were witnessing was not a change of country but a changing of the guard. This was the hour when the prairie was taken over by the creatures of the night, and when at last we moored in a small oil slip some five miles further on, beside two toylike tanks and a little jetty and another of those offices with barred windows and an armor-plated door, one of us whistled and called coaxingly to a furtive dog that came slinking out of the marshes. It was the first dog I had known to ignore a proffered cookie. It slunk away at a stealthy trot along the narrow road to nowhere; after it had vanished in the encroaching darkness there was the long wail of the coyote greeting the night.

That night, each one of us on board was utterly alone, his consciousness wide open and listening in the silence. The first tow that passed us in the darkness came as a relief. It sucked the water right out of the little slip where we were moored and sent it gushing back again like a tidal wave, straining moorings and hawsers; the night was suddenly filled with crashes and bangs, squeals and crunchings and the tremendous gurgle of turbulent water. It was a relief, for it was the end of the silence.

During the rest of the night, many tows passed by and everyone's sleep was fitful; but without them, there would have been no sleep at all.

2 *Louisiana*

CONTENTS

THE ETERNAL FLAME

THE NIGHT after we crossed the border into Louisiana, we were fortunate in our mooring. After a long, arduous day's journey on the Intracoastal Waterway in a strong side wind that blew the many tows of empty barges across the channel, turning navigation into a game of giant dodge-'ems, we arrived at the little slip we had picked out on the chart: a mooring alongside some oil storage tanks in a short channel between the waterway and a big expanse of water called Sweet Lake.

Inside the lake, the chart showed a number of crosses that stood for oil wells; when we arrived that night at dusk, I saw across the silver expanse of one of the most romantic lakes I had ever seen the spidery towers of oil derricks, the low dotted lines of the jetties that linked them, and in the heart of their sparse steel forest the caged bird of a fluttering flame. I had seen similar flames all over Texas; I did not quite know what they stood for or what their function was, all I knew was that they went with oil wells.

The storage tanks alongside which we moored were, as was usual in these slips along the waterway, beautifully kept in silver paint and stood in a lawn that would have graced a mansion. There were paved walks from tank to tank; a little road of flagstones crossed the lawn from the jetty to the low, innocent jungle beyond. Birds came to see us at once with an expectancy that proved that many bargees had fed them during their lonely evenings in the wilderness. We crumbled loaves, chopped nuts and had started to cut cheese cubes, bite-size for a grackle, when darkness fell. There were only two birds among the crowd who refused to have their food cut up for them and sprinkled on the lawn: a couple of nighthawks who swooped and circled overhead, squawking angrily, looking like miniature warplanes with the round white markings under their wings. When it became too dark to see even them, we turned in.

I had, during the trip, taken to leaving the curtains of my cabin open to be awakened by the dawn; that night, despite the quiet, pleasant mooring, I could not fall asleep for on the ceiling there quivered, reflected by the water, the restless flame across the lake. After watching for a while the play of light and shadow on the ceiling, I got up and looked out of the porthole.

In the heart of the darkness the giant candle flame, much brighter now, was dancing and flickering, tugging at its wick; across the lake lay the restless path of its reflection. As I stood staring at it I thought of other flames: the one underneath the Arc de Triomphe in Paris, in Arlington, in most of the capitals of the world, commemorating the Unknown Soldier of the First World War. "Eternal flames," man had called them in his odd conception of time; but since the solemn burial of those unknown soldiers other wars had been fought, more cruel than the first; of the millions who had earnestly echoed the cry, "Lest We Forget!" thirty years ago, only a diminishing band of cantankerous men with old banners and withered slogans were left. After the death of the last one of those, Eternity would have come to an end.

While looking across this black lake on the border of Louisiana at the flame dancing in the darkness, I reflected that if there were life on other planets, further advanced than ours, the first sign to the observer in outer space of the birth of intelligence on our globe would have been the pinpricks of light of man's first campfires in the darkness. It must have been a fascinating sight, the beginning of a story of suspense. If they were watching us now, it would still be this flame they were watching; for although it had leaped from log to furnace, from furnace to derrick, from derrick to atomic pile, it was still the same flame of man's quest for knowledge, precariously caged in the great darkness.

I stopped mourning our short eternity and gazed at the puny candle flame of our courage in the interstellar night with a feeling of hope.

FORKED ISLAND

WE DID not travel on Sundays, and never quite knew beforehand where we would moor for the weekend. This particular weekend we had hoped to spend at Intracoastal City, Louisiana, but we did not get that far. We moored on the Saturday afternoon in an oil slip near a village called Forked Island, just off the waterway.

The small basin was surrounded by surly men in overalls and cowboy hats. As we were tying up, a fat foreman came out of an office and strolled toward us, behaving as if the men were not there. There was an odd tension in the air. The foreman's steps on the gravel sounded loud and so did the buzzing of the bees; if I had closed my eyes, I could have taken him for a stroller in a summer garden. He came closer than was necessary and said, quietly, "Scram, Cap. There's a strike on. This place is picketed, and they ain't in a kidding mood."

"I had hoped I could tie up here for the weekend," I said.

The foreman shook his head. "Nix," he said. "You get out of here, fast. There's a tanker coming to unload them tanks and there's going to be trouble. It'll be here any moment, so, hurry back now." He said the Southern greeting with a sour sense of humor. As he turned round to go back to his office, I saw a revolver in a holster dangling from his belt.

Before we had got to the oil slip, I had spotted a narrow dead-end canal leading off the waterway, with a couple of old barges in it that seemed to be laid up there. I backed out of the little harbor under the stares of the silent men, went back half a mile the way we had come and nosed gingerly into the dead-end channel. The barges were old indeed; their decks had been patched up with concrete as a last resort before they were abandoned. After I had moored alongside one of them I went down into the engine room to turn off the engine; in the sudden silence, I heard through the open hatch the song of a bird.

It was melodious and yet quite wild, a song a skylark might sing once it is out of earshot. I stood there listening, while small noises of cooling water and hot metal bubbled and creaked in the engine. Then I climbed back on deck, cautiously, so as not to disturb the singer. As I looked round, my eyes at the level of the concrete deck of the old barge, I saw the graceful silhouette of an alert young snake staring at me with what seemed amazement. The heavy, drooping summer trees, whose foliage overhung the old barge, seemed to turn it into a Roman garden. All this had been the same centuries and centuries ago, and would remain the same in centuries to come: the snake, the bird, the summer trees; I felt as if in this one moment in eternity the concentric rings of past and future silently crossed. This was Paradise lost and Paradise regained; this was all summer gardens on earth as some distant traveler from another planet would describe them to those at home.

Then there sounded the blast of an air horn, close by. The little snake rustled away; the red flash of a cardinal flitted into the violet shade of the summer trees. Along the canal behind us the dark silhouette of a tanker slowly drifted past.

NIGGER ISLAND

On this particular day we had decided, looking at the chart, that the best mooring was a fairly big slip dug into an isolated patch of marshland called Nigger Island. It was near enough for us to make the run comfortably and be moored well before nightfall.

The Intracoastal Waterway, once broken by the wide and romantic bend of the Vermilion River, never recovered its geometrical aspect. The south bank consisted of small, wild islands overgrown with reeds and mangrove shrubs; here and there were hills on which stood ramshackle farmhouses surrounded by tall trees. Most of the houses were obviously abandoned; their shutters, seen through the binoculars, swung blindly in the wind, their roofs were caved in; the Spanish moss, trailing from the trees like seaweed, made the buildings, veiled by their waving shrouds, seem submerged.

When we came to Nigger Island, we saw another of

those farms that looked like a pleasant white ranch from afar and turned out to be an eerie ruin when approached. The slip we had selected was desolate; three rusty oil tanks, obviously empty, stood starkly etched against the soft green sky of the evening; the dock sagged on rotten pilings; behind the dike lay a pile of rusty equipment overgrown with weeds. Standing on the dock I could see, through the dark alley of a tree-lined drive, the ruins of the farmhouse on its little hill.

The desolation that oozed from this silent scene was such that I hesitated to spend the night there. There was in the atmosphere something beyond evil; as if this scene were a glimpse of purgatory, where the secret sins of forgotten generations are expiated in motionless silence, where past violence is frozen into the eternal torture of the mind.

Then one of us said, "There's people living in that house. I just saw someone looking out of that window."

I asked, "Are you sure?"

He said, "You bet I am," and went to take in the forward mooring.

I took in the aft one; we backed out of the harbor of Nigger Island, and sailed on into the darkening, comforting unknown.

BAYOUS IN THE RAIN

To SAIL the bayous of Louisiana is to visit the past. Not the past of the Indians, the buccaneers, Jean Lafitte and Longfellow's pure girlhood, but the past that would frighten even the alligators and make the great blue heron take off, croaking, in the receding light.

The unimaginable age of the bayous does not suddenly confront the traveler, it grows on him with time. It will take him days, perhaps weeks, before the realization dawns on him that he has wandered into a prehistoric garden, overgrown with weeds. There is about the cypresses standing up to their knees in the water, about the mangroves creating the illusion of land, about the islands of water hyacinths slowly floating downstream, silent and scentless, an inexpressible nostalgia, a static sadness, as if the whole of nature in this alien land were mourning a lost memory. Then the first drops fall from the heavy clouds, and the traveler looks up at the sky. It is raining, just rain; why should this alarm him?

The rain falls and narrows the horizon. The lonely man in his boat finds himself caught in the narrowing net of the jungle. There is around him an awakening; the wind rustles through the wet leaves like a sigh; then he realizes that this is the memory the bayous have been mourning. This is how they were born, this is the comforting sound of their childhood.

Man can look at the stars at night, and reflect upon his futility; he can stand in awe on a crater's edge and realize the eons that went into the planet's creation; but nothing will terrify him like the reality of the bayous in the rain. He is still haunted by the subconscious memory of the Great Flood, and there is one place on earth where this tellurian catastrophe is remembered with joy, like a sleeper awakening. When it rains on the bayous, a wordless voice wanders through the jungle, humming; and the traveler will hold his breath, assailed by the loneliness of Paradise before his creation.

BARATARIA

THE MELANCHOLY world of the Louisiana bayous, which stretches from the Vermilion River in the
west to the Mississippi in the east, has two highways
crossing it from north to south. One is Bayou Lafourche,
a long, narrow river, with houses on both banks for
miles on end, known as the longest village street in the
state; the other is Bayou Barataria, a tortuous stream of
murky brown, stretching from the Intracoastal Waterway in the heart of the bayou country to the sea.

Lafourche is a village street indeed, full of gossip,
large families, dogs of all sizes who all have the pre-
posterously large pointed ears of the chihuahua, and
many shrimp boats; past it all trundles the ice-cream man
in his old white van, ringing the bell that children hear
in their dreams. It is a world of childhood and old
people's memories; between the two there are the pas-
sions, the fights, the loves and the solitudes of manhood
confined to a village street. You could do worse than be
born or retire on the banks of Bayou Lafourche.

Not so its sultry sister, Barataria. The moment a

stranger rounds the bend where Barataria joins the Intracoastal Waterway, he is struck by a change in the
atmosphere. The Intracoastal, straight and impersonal, is
a neutral background to the helmsman's thoughts, and
seems to adapt itself to the key of the melody of his
musings. Bayou Barataria, however, forces its own mood
upon the traveler, and it is neither in a major nor in a
minor key. There is only one word for it—from its beginning to its end in the blue waters of the Gulf it is
hostile.

The hostility seems to emanate from the shores, the
banks of floating hyacinths, the cypress swamps, the old
trees leaning over the black water, garbed with the
shrouds of the Spanish moss as if in mourning. Man,
making his dwelling along its bank, has taken on Barataria's own aspect; the same Cajuns that in Lafourche
are gregarious, talkative, and gay, seem suspicious, somber and taciturn on the banks of Bayou Barataria. There
are many fishermen and shrimpers; there are old boats
dotting the shores in colorful strings; there are villages
with grocery stores and funeral parlors like anywhere
else. The only things there seem to be more of than anywhere else are cemeteries and vultures.

This is a sad country, for hostility and suspicion ir-
revocably lead to isolation. The silent faces staring at
the stranger from the river's banks are the faces of envy.
Not envy of our riches or our freedom, but envy of our
brotherhood.

That night, we moored outside a factory. As the ship's
dog leaped ashore and found at once a caretaker's cat,
two women came running, brandishing carpet beaters.
They were mother and daughter; on seeing the ship,
they forgot about the cat. "Where you from?" they
asked, and when I answered that we were from Hol-

land, their eyes lit up and they said, "How wonderful! We are from Texas."

We had coffee and talked about the world we shared: the wide, happy world beyond the banks of Bayou Barataria.

JUMP UP AND RUN

To THE coastwise sailor the American genius has brought many a blessing. One of them is the direction finder, a small, sensitive radio set with an aerial in its revolving handle that will point up with amazing accuracy the bearing of the radio station it is tuned in to. It will guide the sailor home if only he keeps on the music's beam.

One late afternoon, as Rival was approaching the Louisiana coast hidden in a beautiful but lethal summer haze, I turned on the direction finder and tuned in to a local radio station ashore. By keeping the ship headed in the direction where the volume of the transmission was at its lowest pitch, the station would guide me to one of the entrances of the Mississippi and a safe harbor from the menacing squall astern, which betrayed its presence by crashing and crackling as I turned the radio on.

Staring at the compass and at the golden haze ahead, I found myself listening to a revival meeting, where a preacher seemed to be performing a miracle. From the hoarse exhortations of the ecstatic voice and the tom-tom-like incantation of the congregation, I gathered that a lame girl in a wheel chair was being urged to get up and walk.

The sea was still and eternal; the fleecelike clouds drifted silently toward the night. The ship sailed on with a sleepy motion, safe in what the old sailors called the Hand of God. There was, in the emptiness of the ocean, a great Presence that crashed and crackled in the loud-speaker as the voice of the preacher screamed and whispered, cajoled and pleaded, urging the lame girl to get out of her wheel chair and walk.

The course was east-northeast; the magic box by the side of the steering wheel pointed at the safety of the harbor by its small metallic voice that quacked, "Get up, baby! Get up for Jesus! Get out of that chair and walk!" The choir grunted in the background with throbbing ecstasy, like a rite of spring; while distant lightning crackled and crashed, the preacher swung up another rung of the ladder of exaltation, and shouted, "She's getting up! She's getting up, like Jesus said she would, two thousand years ago!" Then his voice fell, and he said with quivering calm, "But to prove to you that Jesus still lives after two thousand years, to prove to you that He has passed on His powers to His disciples to hallow His name for ever more, I now say to this girl: 'Verily, I say, thou shalt not only arise and walk' "—his voice rose to a scream—" 'Thou shalt jump up and run!' " The lightning crashed with a sound of destruction into the surging jubilation of the choir that chanted "Hallelujah!" and "Praise and Glory!" through the little horn that guided my ship across the silent, shimmering sea.

The preacher's voice got louder; I turned the wheel, the ship's blind bowsprit swung slowly east along the golden haze of the horizon, like a groping finger, and his voice faded. Then he cried, far away, "God! Jesus! Saints! Sinners! Look! Here she comes! She runs!" A falling tree of colossal lightning crashed in the distance, the choir screamed in unchaste confusion; then there sounded the three pips of a time signal and a cheerful voice said, "Here is the news of the hour, on the hour; but before we bring you the world's headlines, first this message." A choir sang, "You'll wonder where the yellow went, When you brush your teeth with Pepsodent," and a gentle, persuading voice started to chat about teeth, gums, bad breath and love.

A shadow passed over the ship. I looked up, and saw the black kite of the first buzzard of the shore.

10 P.M.—RELIGION

In New Orleans we finally succumbed to the temptation of television. A small set was installed in Rival's main cabin and for a few days nobody did a stroke of work.

We watched everything: early-morning cooking sessions, kindergarten, a dressmaking course, the news, "Industry on Parade" and Arthur Godfrey. It was like a drug, for we would not have more than glanced at any of these performances had we seen them in real life. We picked up some useful hints on what to grease our hair with, how to shrink hemorrhoids, how to apply a home perm, and shouting doctors in surgical gowns gave us a view of the engine room inside our heads, full of flashing lights, sledge hammers and a seismograph run wild.

We scanned the newspaper for program information; nobody seemed particularly interested in a 10 P.M. item vaguely called "Religion." But of course we watched it, and suddenly I found myself back on that still, golden afternoon when the direction finder had guided the ship safely home through the haze on the horizon. This time I took part in the miracle of the curing of a child.

Our small crew of friends sat watching the flickering

screen as we had sat for days now, drinking in the subtle drug of expert hucksters. The young evangelist, looking very trim, who proceeded to sell religion on easy terms to his audience, among which we found ourselves included, seemed one of the hucksters. None of us was narrow-minded on the subject of religion but, like most sailors, we hid a deep respect for it and would, on the brink of the great darkness, ask for a man of God rather than for a doctor. The spruce young salesman strutting up and down his little podium put our backs up by the aggressive way in which he tried to sell God and His Son, to whom he referred as "Jesus of Nazareth" in a tone of equality. Then he announced that he would now proceed to his weekly activity of healing the sick.

He beckoned one of his attendants and took off his coat. Around the little flickering image in the cabin of the ship in the darkness of the Louisiana night there was a tightening of jaws, an involuntary clenching of fists. If we had actually been present at his performance, this would have been the moment when we would have walked out. But we went on watching the young colleague of Jesus of Nazareth, as he took a seat on a straight-backed chair at the edge of the podium, pulled down the microphone with an experienced gesture, and called for the first patient. He was handed a card, which he read while we watched the patient approaching.

She was a terrified child of about twelve, her hands crippled by disease. She was led by a woman who must have been her mother, and who had difficulty in holding back her tears. They were approaching the camera with courageous awe; we had the feeling that they were approaching us.

The camera switched back to the preacher, who started to fire off questions at the mother: Did she believe? Had she given her soul to God? What was her

husband's job? How old was the child? What was the
trouble? Arthritic hands? Give me your hands, baby;
let us pray.

The preacher grabbed the child's hands, closed his
eyes, and demanded of his Sponsor to cure this child.
"Come on, God, give this kid a break. Show these people
what religion can do for them." While waiting for the
answer, he opened his eyes and whispered, "It's coming!
Brothers, it's coming!" Then he closed his eyes once
more and went on urging the Almighty to cure this here
child.

While he did so, the camera gave us a view of the
audience, and that view struck us like the fist that had
struck Saul off his horse on the road to Damascus.
There sat a multitude of anonymous people, housewives,
workmen, boys, Negro women, Mexicans—thousands
of listeners to Jesus of Nazareth on the shores of Lake
Galilee, all gazing at the little girl in front of the podium
with anxious attention. They had, for the moment, forgotten about themselves, moved by the miracle of mercy.

The camera switched back to the preacher clutching
the hands of the child; while he went on pleading with
his eyes closed, the child's eyes opened in rapturous
awe as she felt what we felt: the mercy of the multitude
behind her surging toward her like a great wave of love.
She took her hands from the tight fists of the preacher,
stretched them out toward the sky, and they were cured.

While the young salesman crowed triumphantly into
his mike, the camera swept the multitude once more, and
we saw, as in a glass darkly, that during that split second
of Grace we had all contributed to the miracle—all of
us, seen and unseen, except, so it seemed, the preacher,
the only one among the millions who had been unable to
forget about himself.

But then, who were we to judge? Would the multi-

tude have been there without him? What was he: instrument of God, catalyzer of our prayer, medicine
man, tribal magician? Above our wonder, doubt and
anger radiated the smile of the child who, alone among
the millions, had steadfastly believed in the goodness of
man.

THE BIPLANES OF NEW ORLEANS

LAKE PONTCHARTRAIN, at the brink of which New Orleans crouches, has a hard time mirroring the sunset or the mystery of the diamond-flashing night. The moon will not float on its back in its molten darkness, for the lonely boatman who approaches the great city from the lake can see only the conflagration of its lights. The lighthouse blinks pointlessly amidst a profusion of tumbling cascades, spinning wheels, kicking legs, spurting fountains and running messages of light shouting, *Hello Mellow Jax* and *Sweet, Smooth and Sassy.* Even the Coast Guard launch takes its bearing to the harbor on the Wheel of Funland and changes course when it falls in line with the Cascade of Beer. It is the only way to find the lighthouse at night.

The harbor on the lake is restless with lights and their reflection until the dawn. To sit on deck looking at the sky is a strangely depressing experience; nature seems so far, man's loneliness lost. Lake Pontchartrain is like Walden Pond: its spirit has flown before the hordes that came stampeding on their lemminglike quest for solitude.

Then, suddenly, out of the darkness transformed into perpetual dusk by the sleepless merchants' fireworks, there alights on the rigging an elflike creature. It has a long shining body, two very large eyes and four gauze wings: a dragonfly. It seems as if the lake has sent a reassurance: the spirit is still there and may alight secretly for a fleeting moment to console those who mourn its passing. Then there is another tiny rustle of metallic wings, and a second dragonfly alights in front of the first. The shining bodies tremble slightly in the night breeze, the gauze wings quiver. Then there comes a third, a fourth, a dozen, a score; never has the stranger to the city seen so many dragonflies at once, and scant minutes later the spirit of the lake has filled him with awe.

For a hundred dragonflies are astounding, but thousands of them are terrifying. This makes one suddenly realize that the ephemeral creature of this summer's dusk is not the dragonfly but the sleepless merchant, Sweet, Smooth and Sassy, who flashes into the interstellar void his message of Hello Mellow Jax. Yesterday, there rose out of the mangroves and the reeds Meganeura, the mother of these dragonflies, with a wing span of thirty inches, to rattle up into the summer sky, bound for the swamp where snorted Allosaurus, the terrible lizard of whom she alone among living creatures was not afraid.

If that was yesterday, the stranger in the dusk reflects, what day will be tomorrow?

HENRY FORD'S BOAT

BOATS are never worth the money you put into them once you have fallen in love with them. I know a houseboat whose owner told me with pride that she was triple-bottomed, double-hulled, had separate little insulation shields suspended between the inner and the outer walls of her deckhouse and was specially constructed to withstand pack ice. When he was forced to sell the ship because she had ruined him, the amount he finally received, after having descended from the astronomical figure of her original cost, was a shame. But it just so happened that, at the time he was forced to sell, there was no one about who wanted separate little insulation pads hung between the inner and the outer walls of his deckhouse, and travelers by houseboat to the Arctic were rare that season. The man who bought her from him for a song thought he had been very sharp; but a year later he had to admit that the ship he got for so little was bought too dear, because she would never be his. Ships have hearts and they remain unreasonably with the impractical dreamer who spent all his money on her; second owners are always the losers.

In the yacht harbor of New Orleans, I noticed a curious vessel mooring at the dock. Her superstructure, perched on top of an old-fashioned hull, looked very odd. The owner, a determined gentleman, leaped ashore, fastened a bowline, told his wife to fasten the stern one, and explained, "You see, my superstructure has no sharp corners. It is built like a car, rounded and flowing. It cost more money than three new boats put together. And do you know who designed and owned it? The late Henry Ford. I got her for a song."

The old boat's superstructure looked indeed like the top of a big, old-fashioned automobile. There was a unity of ugliness in her, a graceless solidity that bespoke the love of an aging man who never realized, as he sat idly sketching her bulbous lines, that he was in search of beauty. Looking at the odd old ship, I felt that to one man at least she had been beautiful; I also felt that she would never belong to another. She merely tolerated the new owner and his wife who sat glumly watching a television set during their long, lonely evenings on board a boat that wasn't theirs, and never would be.

Henry Ford the First made it his life's motto that utility came before beauty and uniformity before style, but his boat betrayed that the elusive muse had caught up with him in the end.

STREETS OF SIN

BRAVER than Custer's last stand, and more desperate than the struggle for survival on the raft of the Medusa, is the battle that Sin in New Orleans is fighting with the rising tide of respectability engulfing it from the Midwest.

The inhabitants of the French Quarter in New Orleans thought they were on to a good thing when they perpetuated the absinthe houses, the strip-tease honky-tonks and the naughty book shops in the dark alleys adorned with the black lace of cast-iron balconies. But ever since the Bad Men of the Old Far West became the teen-agers' heroes to compensate their earnest desire to go steady, sin has been on the wane on Bourbon Street.

As I walked one summer evening through the garishly lit alleys, where the doors of the dens of vice were left enticingly ajar, I had to adjust my pace to a shuffling crowd of adolescents in bobby socks, jeans and sneakers who peered massively through each opened door at the embarrassed temptress wriggling her hips, thrusting her pelvis and rotating the tassels sewn on to the nipples of her brassiere. They stared until she lost her composure and the tassels their momentum, and the barker shut the door.

Each barker had his own way of coping with the rising tide; some of them brazened it out by shouting at the earnest young crowd from the plains, "Come on in, men, the tassels are turning!" or whispering hoarsely: "Hurry! The fireball's on tonight!" Others were cynical and cried: "Half price, folks! Tonight is Family Night!" But whatever they cried, and despite the courage with which they faced defeat, they were obviously doomed.

The streets of sin in New Orleans are now as sanitized and hygienic as the reptile pavilion in the zoo. The turning tassels, which once set sex-starved cowpokes whinnying like stallions in rut, have become a demonstration of gymnastics; the sequins with mustaches, the bad champagne and the chemical absinthe that once figured so prominently on the posters of the broad and the narrow road in church entrances and temperance halls have vanished; the posters themselves, aged to curios, now adorn the bathrooms of sophisticated young couples.

In the French Quarter of New Orleans, I came to the conclusion that the goal of our younger generation is, once more, respectability. It seemed understandable during the naughty nineties that youth rebelled against the staid morality of the community by sinning; to go to the devil in a brothel, to stake one's virgin sister at poker, to steal one's parents' life savings for the sake of a sultry nude on a tiger skin meant to assert the freedom of the individual, to escape from the anonymous, dun-colored ranks of massive salvation. "Onward Christian Soldiers, Marching as to War" was a song that, like all war songs, brought about deserters.

Then war came, the wanton slaughter of youth in the

first, the six million Jews and the two atom bombs of the second, followed by the powerless demagoguery of the present leaders of the world. Now, so it seemed, the individual guilt of the naughty nineties had turned into the communal guilt of the lunatic fifties. The adolescent of that time, who stalked the twilit streets of New Orleans in drainpipe trousers and with a collar that made the act of looking round a movement of the hips, escaped from the herd by sinning. The teen-agers going steady, who now shuffled through these same streets, endeavored to escape from our communal guilt by individual respectability.

But then, gradually, my slow procession through the alleys of the past with the citizens of tomorrow became an exhilarating experience. The periods in our history during which mankind had felt a communal guilt had been the best: the rungs of the ladder up which man had climbed out of the chasm of animal unconsciousness. During the last of these periods of communal guilt arose, in silent adoration, the splendor of the cathedrals, proffering to heaven their wordless prayer for forgiveness.

That night, as I shuffled with the teen-agers past Pair-a-Dice Bar and Absinthe House ("It's Later than You Think"), I seemed to catch, as I looked up from our dark furrow, the first glimpse of the spires of tomorrow, touched by the flush of a new dawn.

THE RABBITS OF KILONA

Outside New Orleans, somewhere along the banks of the Mississippi, there is a place of entertainment advertised by billboards for miles ahead called KILONA'S SNAKE FARM—HOME OF THE WILD.

The drive north along the Mississippi levee from New Orleans is a regression in time, a return into the past, not only of America but of mankind. The stately homes with their pillared porches at the far end of gold and green alleys of sunlight and shade contrast quaintly with the Negroes' hovels; the cars of white families covering weary Negro pedestrians with dust along the summer road seem oddly close to *Uncle Tom's Cabin.* And when you arrive at Kilona's Snake Farm, Home of the Wild, the trail mankind left behind on its quest for humanity plummets down several eons into a strangely harsh-lit clearing in the woods, where primitive man with mindless mirth did things to living animals that are better not remembered.

The snake farm looks cheerful from the outside; there is popcorn and Coca-Cola and a young girl in a flowered cotton dress in the ticket booth. Inside, a happy crowd of sight-seers in colored shirts lift cameras and children to peer over the edge of the snake pit where, in the stark concrete depths, lie, somnolently coiled, man's earliest tempters. The scene is one of repose; but for the smell, the cheerfulness outside would persist. Along the walls are cages with little mammals, all in different stages of moulting; a door leads to a sunlit yard in which there are more concrete pits, this time filled with alligators.

The relief you feel at stepping outside into the yard is so striking that it is tinged with alarm. Why this sudden feeling that leaving the snake pit is an escape from evil? It is incomprehensible; but soon your attention is distracted by the antics of a youth among the alligators. There are the prehistoric monsters, in stagnant pools full of their excrement, and there is the young man who grew up among them: an obese adolescent who somehow looks obscene among his captives, slapping them on the rump, kicking their snouts and bawling, "Come on out, ah'll rip yer to pieces! Come on out, I dare yah!" while women giggle with fright and male cameras are whirring. After watching this spectacle for some minutes it begins to lack luster and you turn to leave, for this is all there is to be seen in Kilona's Home of the Wild. To reach the exit, you have to pass the snake pit once more, and the moment you cross the threshold that eerie spell is thrown over you again: a constriction of the throat, a primeval sense of evil, a twinge of inexpressible fear. You hurry to the doorway, behind which sunlight shimmers on car roofs and where the flaxen-haired girl in the ticket booth sits bent, chewing, over a novel. Then, as you hurry toward that small framed picture of cheer and safety, you see them.

Huddled against the wall, at the bottom of the snake pit, are two live rabbits. One, a white one, is lying half on its side as if dead, but its eyes are open in unimaginable terror. It is the kind of rabbit associated with childhood and sunny lawns.

The other is the hare Albrecht Dürer drew. It sits there exactly as he saw it four centuries ago: motionless, serene in ultimate resignation; and at last you understand the undying beauty of that image.

MR. WADLOW'S ESTATE

SOMEWHERE on the banks of the Mississippi stands a stately home with pillared porch, dappled oak alley and a spacious lawn, on which magnolias shed their heavy-lidded blossoms on a sad old dog snoring among the fallen flowers. The home is open to visitors on Sundays, though a family is in residence; the admission charge of one dollar is levied at the entrance by a charming young boy in knickerbockers who sits reading a novel on a leather sofa, and who is possibly the last polite boy in the South.

The house has a charming atmosphere of family life induced by the closed doors marked PRIVATE rather than by the open ones, which are barred by a rope and show fourposters with patchwork quilts and sitting rooms with antimacassars and scowling ancestors on the walls. There is a guide in the shape of an overpowering lady who waits until the number of visitors meets her approval and then starts to guide them up the stairs which she mounts slowly, one step at a time. One is asked to observe a litho that depicts an Arcadian scene of happy pickaninnies gamboling on the same lawn where the old dog now snores, under the benevolent gaze of a gentleman in white with an imposing beard to hide his generous heart. The lady, joining feet on each step, extols the praises of the past in a voice that echoes in the marble halls. The sight-seers agree with earnest nods and reverent looks at the lithos; as the first bedroom is shown the lady announces, "Mr. Wadlow once carried his bride across this threshold like a fluttering bird." A door marked PRIVATE is opened and an old lady shuffles toward another door marked PRIVATE at the far end of the hall. The sight-seers try to catch a surreptitious glimpse of the truth behind the door, and see a fourposter, an air-conditioner, and back issues of *Life*. "Yes!" the lady shouts to recapture the attention. "Those were the days! Let us now go to the balcony and gaze upon the sight Mr. Wadlow's bride saw when she opened the curtains the next morning." She guides the bevy of visitors to the balcony, where they gaze down upon the avenue of oaks. Between two trees is a child's swing, and somebody has again forgotten to take his tricycle in. In the distance is the levee of the Mississippi. "If that were not there," the lady explains resonantly, "you could see the river."

After the tour of the balcony those who still have breath left may go and cast a look round the attic, but are warned that it is very hot. On the wall of the stairs leading up to the attic is an old map of the neighborhood, showing all the estates in the days before the carpetbaggers. You see, to your amazement, that among the big and prosperous plantations there is a very narrow one, smaller than any of the others, called "Mr. Wadlow's Estate"; only then do you realize the grandeur that has gone.

The attic is dark and indeed very hot and it has a strange timelessness, a last link with the past. There are rickety old cane chairs stacked in angular profusion and covered with dust. There is a row of cracked saddles over a beam, and there, in the slanting sheaf of late sun-light alive with gold dust, is a globe which, when turned by a reverent hand, reveals the gay colors of forgotten Empires and Confederacies, Unions and Caliphates, and in the heart of Africa the white unknown, into which Stanley has not yet ventured to recapture Livingstone. The banks of the Mississippi are tinged with red, the blood-red dawn the young bride saw when she opened the curtains the next morning.

DR. LAVERGE OF WAGGERMAN

SOMEWHERE on the Mississippi, not far from
New Orleans, there is a village called Waggerman, the
population of which consists almost entirely of Negroes.
I stopped my rented car to consult the map with which
a gas-station attendant had provided me; as I looked up
to find out the name of the street on which I had stopped,
I noticed a nameplate saying DR. LAVERGE, SURGEON, and
thirty-five years fell out of my past.

I played again in the Oosterpark Street in Amsterdam,
wearing a peaked cap back to front, blowing up a paper
bag to explode it in the echoing porch of an old spinster's
house. Dr. Laverge, a venerable patriarch with a white
beard and a stovepipe hat, caught me as I darted, jubilant,
from the porch, after the spinster had leapt back screaming, slamming the door. Dr. Laverge, who had brought
me into the world and given me my first hiding upside
down to provoke my first thin squeal, now grabbed me
by the ear and led me back to our own front door where
he pulled the bell with the hook of his umbrella. My
mother opened the door and stared at me in horror as

Dr. Laverge described my exploit. When I looked round desperately for a way out I caught a glimpse of his stern and venerable face in the mirror over the umbrella stand, and saw to my astonishment that, underneath the mask of his thinning beard, he was smiling.

Years later, when my mother and I were rummaging through old photographs in a trunk in the attic, she held up a negative against the light and cried, "Look! I think this is Doctor Laverge!" I looked, and indeed, there he was: in a white hat, with a black face and a black beard; my last glimpse of the old man was a negative that had turned him into a Negro. And now, here was his name again: on a door in Waggerman, Louisiana.

From that moment, my eyes were opened to a magic world of remembrance. I got out of the car, walked the streets of Waggerman, and as I did so I saw all around me the negatives of old friends, leaning out of windows, smiling behind counters, laughing on porches, and I felt overcome by a feeling of joy and inexpressible relief, as if a gnome had thrown a spell over me under which I seemed to move in a world of kindness, friendship and love.

I spent hours in the village; when I stood on the crown of the levee, looking at Old Man River, I suddenly heard a click behind me. I turned round and saw a little Negro boy holding a brand-new box camera, grinning at me with a triumphant smile, before he ran off, crying, "Ma, ma, ah shot a snap!"

Never since have I been able to discuss the color question without a guilty lack of concentration. For in the midst of all the serious talk I suddenly see a Negro youth in an attic, holding up an old negative to the light, and I hear him ask, "Who's that, for Pete's sake?" After looking with a frown at the little black man on the crown of the white dike, his mother cries, "Why! That's the first picture you took! That man on the levee, years ago, remember?"

I am sure he won't remember; but then, man today should not try to live tomorrow. He should be content to silently watch its dawn.

A YOUNG LOVER

HE CAME on board in New Orleans, brought by a cheerful friend who was going to sail with us across the Gulf of Mexico as a member of the crew. "He is wonderful to have on board," the cheerful friend had said, describing him the night before. "He is a member of the motorboat squadron, knows all the knots and has time to spare. He is just ideal."

The ideal young sailor was charming in a dreamy, absent-minded way. He seemed, at first sight, slightly out of place and time. He should have been dressed in a gold-stitched doublet and a feather-plumed beret, leaning over the rail of the Rialto one summer's eve in 1592. He was so obviously in love that his preoccupation seemed almost tragic, as if he had a premonition of the fate waiting for him: the hired assassin, lurking in the dusk at the far end of the bridge, paid in advance in well-used doubloons by his enamorata's husband.

He obviously felt ill at ease, and it turned out he was torn between the desire to make the voyage with us and the sweet obligation he had to take his girl friend back from college to Paris, Tennessee, for the summer vacation. The cheerful friend who sponsored him said, "Come, come, this is a chance you'll only get once in a lifetime! If you don't come for this trip, you throw away your happiness forever. It's the thin end of the wedge. Once you let her have her way, you're done for."

The young lover jutted out his chin, heaved a virile sigh, stretched out his hand toward me and said, "Of course, you're right. Captain, put it there."

We shook hands; he said, "Well, that's settled! Where do we go from here?" and I outlined the trip.

The next morning, the cheerful friend and his wife turned up with a gloomy mien. "That damn fool!" he said. "He was out with his girl last night and had himself convinced again that he should take her home. All women should be shot." His pregnant wife smiled seraphically in the background. It was agreed that I should forget about the faithless lover and behave as if he were not there, even if he should turn up to apologize, which he was sure to do unless that girl had turned him into an utter coward.

He turned up that evening, looking more Raphaelian than before. His love now hung around him like a dark velvet cloak, and he seemed to have paled and elongated overnight. Obviously he was on his way to, or had just come from, the balcony scene. "I'm wretchedly sorry," he said, "but . . ." I told him not to worry, that it was perfectly understandable, and we had a drink. After three drinks, he stretched out his hand toward me, I put it there and outlined the trip once more. "Yes!" he said, as he bent over the chart, "I think you guys may well have saved my life! Any woman who wants a man to pass up a chance like this for a five-hundred-mile drive is not worth . . ." He groped for a value and I helped him out by saying, "Now, after Apalachicola, we get the big jump."

The next morning our cheerful friend, as he loomed on the gangway, looked a picture of doom. "I never want to hear his name again," he said. "He deserves to be forgotten. He has left for Tennessee, secretly, the skunk."

He was forgotten, or so it seemed. His name was not mentioned again; the next morning the ship vanished over the horizon, taking with her the well-kept secret of our envy. For all of us knew in our hearts that his drive with his girl friend would be more adventurous than our journey could ever be, even if we were to be shipwrecked by Sinbad's gale and find, on the silver beach of Apalachicola, Aladdin's treasure shimmering in the sand.

3 *Florida*

CONTENTS

STARFISH

WE ARRIVED in a small fishing port after a voyage of four days and three nights from New Orleans. Darkness was gathering over the wooded horizon as we moored among the shrimp boats, edging our way cautiously into the tidal current. There was no one about on either the boats or the dockside, and we realized it was Saturday night.

There is nothing quite like mooring a ship after a solitary journey through day and night, sun and rain, the evening haze and the blue mist of the morning; even after a voyage of only a few days the shore seems strangely precious, Paradise regained.

Paradise, in this case, was an old wooden warehouse with a sagging jetty. Most of the mooring poles were unsafe; there was a brackish smell in the air of dead fish and seaweed bared by the tide; on the door of the warehouse, blistered by the sun, a notice was tacked saying something about the prices of shrimp. On the corner of the dock lay three large shells that smelled strongly and a small dead starfish. We filed ashore, happy, relieved and full of anticipation, for at the far end of the dark alley between the buildings there were neon lights and the flashing colors of passing cars.

We found an old-fashioned hotel with a big gloomy hall full of chintzy chairs and a bar attended by an old Viennese. The old Viennese was drunk, but grandly so. His gestures as he uncorked bottles were full of graceful resignation to the fact that, instead of catcalling at modern opera in the Vienna Burg Theatre, he was condemned to pour rum and Coca-Cola for rowdy barbarians home from the sea. It all turned into a very pleasant evening and we decided it was a pity we could not stay longer than these few hours, that we had to sail again at high tide. As we made our way back toward the dark edge of the town where the river swirled, the idea of setting out to sea again was filled with sadness, for we had just skimmed the surface of the delights of the land. It seemed sadly inadequate that all we had to take home in our treasure chest of memories of this little town was an old Viennese, uncorking a bottle and saying, "Ach, if I vere to tell you . . ."

We groped our way through the black alley between the buildings to the blacker darkness beyond, to the stench of fish and tide. And then, as we climbed onto the dark dock, there lay, in the corner, like a gem at the end of a pilgrimage, the little starfish, luminous in the night.

THE BIG JUMP

THERE is in the chain of protected inland waterways that joins Brownsville, Texas, with New York,
one weak link: the crossing of the Gulf of Mexico between Apalachicola and Tarpon Springs. For the Intracoastal Waterway stops at the fishing port in northwest
Florida to start again in the Greek sponge-fishers' village
some two hundred miles to the south. There are plans
to dig a canal along Florida's coast, but so far they are
plans only. The mariner who wants to sail from Mexico
to New York with a river craft has to face the elements
during the two hundred miles of what is known as The
Big Jump.

It is a big jump indeed, for in two days and one night
you sail from one planet to another. Apalachicola is the
last outpost of a world heavy with the scent of man,
wild and unbridled as nature may be in places. The
Southern states, from Texas to Alabama and even northern Florida, carry the memory of generations of colo-
nists, warriors and slaves. Tarpon Springs, however,
which is reached after a restless voyage of squalls and
thunder and broiling heat exploding into steaming rain,
turns out to be a trading post on the brink of an un-

conquered continent. Nowhere in the South is man's presence felt to be so ephemeral, nowhere do the houses look so much like glorified nomads' tents. There is about Florida's west coast an atmosphere of retarded creation that fills the newcomer with bewildered wariness. Nothing seems old: there are no rocks to suggest the age of the earth with their cragged faces, all there is is sand, shells and colonies of birds that are unimpressed by the passing ship. You might have wandered into one of those legendary regions on the other side of the globe that travelers wrote about in the parchment volumes of bygone centuries: the land of the unicorn, the lair of huge secret animals that escaped the Flood. Perhaps this is the keynote of the Florida peninsula, which already filled the first Spanish explorers with a weird prehistoric awe: it is a country that has escaped the Great Flood and awaits its recurrence. In the low, close-cropped jungle man senses the presence of unknown species that fill him with apprehension, because he is not linked with them by the ancient comradeship of Noah's Ark.

Everywhere else in the world, even in darkest Africa, man feels that the animosity between himself and the beasts of prey is a misunderstanding. There must be some way to recover the thin and delicate thread of collective memory that will guide them back to that great shared adventure, when they were both tossed and buffeted on the raging seas of God's wrath, together with thousands of their shipmates in the big, creaking, lumbering Ark. Behind the cold jewels of the tiger's stare there is still caught, in the depth of the dark iris, the image of old Noah's bent little body, and in the silence between heartbeats there still echoes the shrill bickering of Noah's wife, and the cooing of the dove that was to bring the twig of hope in playful innocence.

But when the first frog of the evening begins its toneless bleat in Florida's squatting wilderness, there is no other link between the past of man and beast than God's initial spark, that lit the lights of the universe in the darkness of timeless space.

A BOS'N

When we arrived in the yacht harbor, there was the usual crowd on the dock by the gasoline pumps: the harbor master in khaki with a peaked cap, a couple of young boys in old blue jeans cut off above the knees, with crew-cuts and open mouths, and half a dozen pregnant men. We had had long conversations about what it was in the American diet that gave most of its middle-aged males this maternal appearance, but the conversations had remained without issue. This time I wondered, as I had wondered before, which of those men I would come to know best. I was sure to know one better than the others by the time we left, because this was what had happened in all ports so far.

He was swarthy, aggressive and handsome in a flaccid, overripe way, like a heavy rose about to droop. He ran a party boat: a score of daytime trippers each morning who caught the usual sad collection of useless fish, which were hung on a rack with hooks on the dockside with a chalk-written notice: CAUGHT BY THE PARTY ON BOARD MISS UNIVERSE, to stink through the night, dripping blood and primeval ooze, until they were carted away in a wheelbarrow by the Negro of the dawn.

My new friend offered to take me into the town in his
car to do some shopping, and as we careened along in
his old Buick that smelled of cats, he told me with New
Worldly frankness about his time in the Navy, his marriage, his divorce; all he was waiting for now was the
custody of his child after the court had saved it from
the clutches of that whore. He was very helpful in keeping the prices down in the shops we visited by the sheer
menace of his khaki-clad bulk, and by the angle of his
peaked cap on the back of his head, which was reminiscent of a corrupt cop. As a matter of fact, that was the
impression that remained: a big man who had set out in
life by submitting to law and order, then had come to
dispense law and order himself, and had gone to seed in
the process. His most illuminating remark during the
short time I knew him was, "If only I had stayed an
ordinary seaman."

The local chief of police and he had known one another in the Navy during the war, when the chief was a
lieutenant and my friend a bos'n. They carried on in the
backslapping democratic way that was expected of them
and yet it was obvious that they couldn't stand the sight
of one another; but then, the bos'n couldn't stand the
sight of anybody much. He referred to his daily passengers as suckers, his fellow townsmen as robbers and
hypocrites, womanhood as a world-wide maffia and
himself as a lost soul. There was a tragic bravura in the
way he flung about the pieces of a cheap broken culture
by saying, "How many sons had Alexander?" and
" 'Keep moving!' as Copernicus said." I ended by avoid-
ing him on the pretext that he was a bore, but what I
really shied away from was the dark vortex of his despair. As we left, he was standing on the fuel dock once
more, a pregnant man in the sunrise, and he waved at

us. But his heart wasn't in it, for he waved good-by at yet another promise that had gone unfulfilled, and stood there waiting for the next one to rise, specklike, from the horizon.

YOO-HOO!

AFTER the big jump across the Gulf one thing had become obvious: the little stray dog that had stowed away on the ship in New Orleans would have to go. During the bad weather at sea several members of the crew had narrowly escaped having their legs broken as they skidded, cursing, on the little dog's traces, and the little dog itself had nearly been beheaded as it stuck its head playfully between the spokes of the steering wheel. So when the local press emerged in the shape of a tough photographer and a poetic young reporter in a sailing cap, I begged them to include in their interview with the captain of the quaint Dutch craft a plea to dog lovers among their readers to collect the puppy and give it a good home. I had myself photographed with it, trying to make it look engaging by surreptitiously pushing up its ears, which had a tendency to flatten. The result in the evening paper looked slightly alarming, but the young poet had put into the plea for the canine orphan a bit of his lonely soul.

I was sure that scores of people would turn up and vie for the pup which was called a "Cajun terrier" in the interview, and described as an Einstein among dogs. But nobody came, until late the following afternoon.

From the crowd that stood permanently looking at the ship from the quayside, there emerged an elderly couple who attracted my attention by shouts and the waving of a newspaper. I went ashore and the lady, with harrowed eyes, asked, "It hasn't been given away yet, has it? Please say it hasn't!" I assured her that she was lucky and that the little dog was still available, at which she heaved a sigh of relief and shouted to her husband, "Darling, we have a new baby!" The husband remained unruffled and presented himself stoically, while the lady opened her purse and brought out an accordion of photographs of dogs. There were poodles with bows, chihuahuas with the round eyes of terror, bulldogs slavering at the sight of the photographer's calves and Doberman pinschers with the frank virility of Papuans. "All these darlings were once ours," the lady cooed, her pale blue, slightly protruding eyes filled with tears. "Now they all have their own individual little grave and a granite headstone with their name on it in the pet cemetery on Route 19. Do you know it?"

I said, engagingly, that I was quite new here, but would hasten to go and have a look at the earliest opportunity. Then the lady asked, "Where is it? Please, where is it?" As she stood biting back tears of expectation, I went and dragged the reluctant puppy from under the mast winch where it had hidden with canine second sight. As it was carried down the gangway by its shoulders, the lady whipped out a lorgnette, peered at the pale babyish belly and said, "Oh . . . A little girl, is it?"

I said it was, but well, in America there were ways

and means to turn little boys and little girls into little
neuters. The lady said, "Oh no, never!" The husband
grunted, "Come, come, Anthea. It's done before you
can say knife."

"Well," said the lady, with a sigh. "We'll discuss all
that later. We just have to pop round and see some
friends first, and then, on our way back, we'll come and
collect the little darling. Now if you are not outside,
how do we attract your attention?"

"Oh," I said, "just call."

"How romantic!" she cried. "Must I call 'Ahoy!' or
just 'Yoo-Hoo!'?"

I said that any call would do. I would be waiting.

"All right," she said. "We'll be back shortly, and I'll
call 'Yoo-Hoo!' Good-by, little darling, mummy won't
be long."

The Einstein among dogs pranced back on board,
ears cocked, tail wagging, and curled up on the helmsman's platform, her head between the spokes of the
wheel. There she remained, blissfully unconcerned,
until we sailed, while Homo Sapiens indoors sat patiently
waiting for the call "Yoo-Hoo." It obviously did not
bother her that she had passed up a perfectly beautiful
tombstone.

AN ELDERLY COUPLE

FLORIDA is advertised throughout the New World as the ideal place for retirement. Its climate, so the folders say, is lenient, its atmosphere soothing and its people real friendly; as a result there are many elderly couples in this sweltering jungle where, on moonlit nights, the earth quivers and the palms rustle eerily as if, somewhere in the swamp, dinosaur and archeopagus were still at play.

One sees them all over Florida, brisk or slow, shuffling cautiously or striding ramrodlike in well-worn sandals, and one among those thousands of elderly couples lives on a boat the husband built himself, and they call one another Skipper and Mate. I never found out what his profession had been before he retired, but it had not been shipwright. He was thin and brisk; she was tiny and birdlike, but rather like a bird treading cautiously on the first ice of winter. They invited us for a drive because, so the Skipper said with a tone of finality, "you cannot just skirt around this place; someone must show you people the heart of Florida."

The car was old but cosily so and adapted by the Skipper to their personal needs. On the steering column was a contraption holding sulphur matches with which he could light his pipe without releasing the wheel; his

pipe was of the kind that refused to draw so he used a lot
of matches during the trip, filling the car with the stench
of brimstone. She sat beside him, her head barely visible
over the edge of the seat; he had rigged up a special
sunshade for her: a second flap attached to the sun visor;
when lowered, it completely blotted out the landscape
for those sitting behind.

Perhaps because of the double flap, or because of the
rain that soon started to fall in tropical profusion, I
concentrated more on observing them than on observing
Florida, hazily reeling past behind the steamed-up windows. She seemed to get older as the trip wore on, worn
out by his aggressive youthfulness as he struck match
after match, bellowed statistics about citrus groves,
shouted with laughter at his own jokes and sang ribald
songs, pounding the old steering wheel with a delicately
veined fist. Her ears seemed to grow bigger as she
sagged, exhausted, cloistered in this iron box on wheels
with her rambunctious skipper who defiantly refused
to grow old.

The heart of Florida turned out to be a tower with an
electronic carillon, erected over a restaurant which, in
its turn, was erected over the grave of a man who had
made a fortune there. She refused to get out in the rain
to look at it; they bickered; when in the end he went
alone he waded through the puddles demonstratively.
The carillon gonged "Come All Ye Faithful" in the rain.
While we sat waiting for his return she talked about
him: what a wonderful man he was, and so good with his
hands, and so courageous and always in high spirits; the
best proof of how full their lives were was that they
didn't feel the need of any pets to keep them company.

He came back, splashing grimly through the puddles,
got in, slammed the door, struck a soot-belching match,
started the engine and backed the car into the rain with a

breath-taking swoop. We drove home along a crowded highway, where we were sprayed with mud by younger cars dashing past. In the end he had to come to a stop, as she had begged him to do for over an hour, and let her out at a roadside cafe while he cleaned the windshield. "Won't you come in and have a cup of coffee?" she asked, but he shook his head with relish. "You go and do what you have to do," he said. "We'll wait out here." Then he grunted, staring at her receding back, "Wonderful woman." During the five minutes that followed, he repeated about her what she had said about him.

Finally, the rain stopped. We were on the crown of a hill. Below us lay the harbor, shining toylike in the glistening light of the evening, and before us, across the Gulf, was the sunset which seemed cavernous and cold, despite its colors. He seemed to hesitate; she put her head on his shoulder. He champed on his pipe with pugnacious pride, and we soared down the hill toward the end of the day, home from our quest for Florida's heart.

THE LITTLE SPOON

THE MAIN effect of crossing the Atlantic by plane is that it dislodges the traveler from time. When I arrived at Idlewild Airport on my first visit to the United States some years ago, after landing at Shannon and Gander, I no longer had any idea of mealtimes by which, so I found, my life had been regulated. Day had turned into night, the sea into land, and in the waiting room, where I ended up after passing through Immigration and Customs, I could buy the same pocket books and the same souvenirs that were on sale in Gander and Shannon. Ireland, Canada, the United States . . . All this was hearsay; the reality was a chromium and Formica bar, a coffee machine, a preoccupied waitress, and a revolving bookstand displaying *Woman's Medical Problems* and *Come and Be Killed.*

Normally, the newcomer to the American shores goes on from there to his first impressions of America: the marvel of New York, the cloying perfume of American after-shave lotion and the television set in the hotel room. In my case, first impressions were postponed, for I took to the air again in a private plane and landed after a hair-raising ride through hail-filled thunderclouds at

Waterville, Maine, where I was to take a train to my eventual destination. So the first impression of the country, after the wild ducks at Idlewild that I spotted as we took off, was a field of yellow flowers when we touched down on a disused military airstrip. The airstrip seemed immense, the prairie of yellow flowers boundless, the walk from the plane to the waiting cab much longer than anywhere else in the world. For a few minutes I was alone with my little suitcase underneath a tremendous, angry sky, trotting nervously along an asphalt road half a mile wide toward a tiny taxi in the distance.

The taxi took me to a railway station. Ticket window, concrete steps, platform in the gathering dusk; I had been in stations exactly like this hundreds of times, and yet this was America, the New World. I walked down the platform behind a family of father, mother and little fat son. As we walked, I noticed a small red object lying on the ground: a little plastic spoon. As I stooped to pick it up, thinking someone must have lost it, the little fat boy pulled himself free from his father's hand, side-stepped, crushed the little spoon with his foot and walked on, his hand back in his father's. I was in America.

Years later, in Florida, I broke a wooden shoe while washing the deck and threw the odd one overboard. As I did so, there was a sharp cry from the dock, a woman crying "No!" When I saw her horrified face, I grinned apologetically and said, "It's no use, you know. I broke the other one." She did not smile, but turned round and hurried away. Some minutes later I heard the roar of a speedboat and saw her flash past with wings of silver foam. She was going to fish out the clog.

First impressions are difficult to overcome, because the image is so vivid in your memory. That's why I now have a drawerful of orphaned little plastic spoons, collected from beach and sidewalk, and a lady in Clearwater has, on the wall of her patio, a wooden shoe filled with tulips: Dixie's silent reproach to the Dutch.

ON LANDING

To GET the true impression of the continent of America, you should not land from boat or plane, nor cross the border by train or automobile, or even on foot.

You should wade ashore, a shipwrecked sailor, through the lazy surf of the Gulf of Mexico and arrive on Florida's prehistoric and eternally youthful beach. The jungle fringe around that big blue water never has time to grow up into maturity; every thirty years or so a hurricane-lashed tidal wave shears all vegetation off the low-lying land except the roots of the mangroves, so the human being wading out of the sea will not confront a rioting jungle, but the aftermath of a disaster.

This is America: the eternal impermanence of any living being, be it plant, beast or man, under the lurking menace of cosmic forces about to raze the table of creation once more. And what is newly created after the catastrophe is but the image of what went before: a neutral adolescent growth of green and flesh, living in constant awareness of the clouds of fury gathering again beyond the horizon.

Nowhere on these shores, or even in the plains and the valleys beyond, has man imposed his will with any semblance of permanence. No continent on earth has higher towers, longer bridges, bigger dams; yet they fail to impress man as monuments of his might. For even the firecracker of his atom bomb is put to ridicule by the black vortex of the twister, reaching up into the sky, by the colossal thunder of the subtropic lowlands, by the tidal waves that crumble houses and turn the roofs of churches into flotsam.

America, when approached from the sea, on foot, alone, shows itself in its true nature as the New World. Although it is as old as the rest of the earth, it is unlike any world man has known and conquered so far. It is unconquered, and will remain so until man has found a new relationship, a new humility and a new might by a total conversion. In this land of hostile nature, of tornadoes, hurricanes, poison oak and poison ivy, where each holiday may end in death, each boat ride in disaster, each nature ramble in poisoned agony, man needs another God than the one he tamed in the old country, where the Holy Ghost is safely enshrined in spired prisons, garlanded with ageless art.

In the heart of Florida is a large, mysterious lake which hurricanes turn into a seething cauldron of destruction, and which between these cosmic spasms lies shimmering in a silver haze. It is now called Lake Okeechobee, Big Water, but the Spaniards when they first arrived gave the unexplored swamp of which the lake was part the name Lake of the Holy Ghost. Although the name of the lake has changed, the Spirit still moves upon its waters, and nature lies waiting for its liberation from fear in the soul of a new, still uncreated man.

AN EGRET

To WALK along west Florida's white, deserted beaches is about the loneliest walk a man can make. For apart from small sections, sparsely sown and far apart, where the tourist bathes because he can get there by car, this is virgin territory.

Yet life is abundant on those beaches. Each wave of the gentle silver surf is the outpouring of a cornucopia, a shower of wriggling little fish, minute multicolored shells and, occasionally, bright orange marvels from the deep that turn brown and putrid within an hour. The jungle beyond the beach is teeming with life also. The frogs rattle, the mockingbird warbles, the rabbits rustle in the shrubs, and between the two worlds of sea and jungle there is a secret flitting traffic of ghostly sand crabs, rapid turtles and the cumbersome pelican, prehistoric policeman on his beat.

Only after making the same walk many times does today's Robinson Crusoe discover that indeed the pelican has its beat, and not only the pelican, but all the birds in this gay profusion of feather, fur and glistening scale have their own well-established routines. I was accompanied each day, for weeks on end, by a little white egret that joined me for my walk at the second palm on a certain point and left me at the first sea wall of the town

of Venice, to fly back to the palm, three and a half miles to the south. The little egret was not shy; as I walked with it day after day and marveled at its brilliant plumage, its graceful gait, its proud slow flight, its dignified independence, I found in its presence America's praise.

For a generation ago the white egret was almost destroyed, as womanhood adorned its ungainly toques with the plumes of the wild bird's parenthood. Only during the nesting season could the egret be approached close enough for the kill, and then not until the eggs were hatched; so each plume on America's millions of toques stood for a murdered parent and an abandoned nest of squealing young, whose thin cries faded into silence. The hired assassins who carried out this extermination were called "millinery agents" and the fact that by now it is they who are extinct and not the white egret is a triumph of the American conscience. For there lived in the South a man called Avery, who made out of an island in the Louisiana swamps a sanctuary for the snowy egret. He hired poachers to defend his island against the millinery agents, and he built complicated contraptions to lure the birds to nest there.

The interested visitor who sees the remnants of these contraptions today realizes at a glance that it was not man who lured the snowy egrets to their highly uncomfortable scaffolds, but God who sent them there. For what was saved on Avery Island was not the snowy egret. That is, after all, replaceable.

A MOONLIT NIGHT

A MOONLIT summer night on Florida's west coast
is different from anywhere else in the world. Full moon
in the Far East, when it rises large and red out of the
scented profusion of the jungle, is a magical occurrence.
It seems, there, as if the animal kingdom down to the
smallest marauders of the night are blessed, during a few
fleeting hours, with a human individuality. The moonlit
garden sings, warbles, laughs and chuckles with feverish
joy, and the listener to this Midsummer Night's Dream
is overcome by a feeling of elation. The rustling, leaping,
laughing and applauding around him fills him with hope;
it seems as if the animals were lifted out of their fearsome
darkness by the touch of a magic wand and allowed to
perceive, as through a glass darkly, the light of consciousness at the end of evolution.

The Florida jungle, recently regrown after the last
hurricane's destruction, has a different atmosphere. As
the moon rises, oval and orange, over the undergrowth
without trees or flowers, the young wilderness is heard
to awaken. The first sound is a distant bleating, as if a
herd of goats were wandering near through the shrubs.

But they are not goats dreaming to be men, they are frogs dreaming to be goats; and as the moon rises higher, there rise with it other sounds in the eerie night, sounds that seem elementary, the sound of life awakening in matter. The close-cropped shrubs, the shorn mangroves, the crippled palms are given voice, and what they express is not hope, but terror.

It is not the terror of evil, nor the ancient terror of the hunted prey in the moonlight. It is basest nature squeaking, squealing, lowing and bleating in an agony of birth, and what terrifies man in this cauldron of creation is the knowledge of what is to come. For in the Florida jungle on the Gulf of Mexico the Great Flood is still in the future.

After the door and the shutters are closed and the lamp is lit, the spell does not abate. Man stands in his cabin, listening, and knows with prehistoric intuition that in the darkness of eons to come there is another disaster, waiting for this planet Earth to swing, blindly, into its rising tide.

THE WATERS
OF VENICE

ON MY walks along the beach and through the houseless, weed-grown streets of South Venice, an abandoned subdivision of the Great Boom, I saw many small openings in the jungle which, on close inspection, turned out to be little waterways. In the end the temptation to explore them became so great that I procured a canoe, which could be strapped on to the roof of the secondhand car I had bought, and set out to investigate. On the village square, where rusty old signs still tried to call the jungle "Oxford Circus," I unstrapped the canoe, carried it through the mangroves to the bank of a streamlet, got in, and with two strokes of the paddle I slid silently from my familiar reality of past, present and future into a timeless no man's land, as if I had inadvertently opened a door to another world. The jungle on the banks of the narrow, winding stream was not in itself surprising or exciting; there was just the unshakable certainty, which had assailed me from nowhere, that I was the first man ever to visit this corner of the earth.

Of course, this was nonsense. Hundreds of people, over the centuries, must have wandered into these narrow backwaters of west Florida, even when it was still called something else. But reason could not dispel that eerie certainty: I was the first, no one had ever been here before me. Then, as I silently drifted deeper into this miniature maze, I felt as if I were growing bigger. The shrubs became lower and the little stream narrower, and it began to dawn on me that my predecessors, if any, must have been young boys, for no man in his senses would waste his time worming his way into this rabbit warren of muddy water and overheated shrub. No animal of any value would hide itself here, fish could much better be caught in the bay where they had room to grow, this was a world of useless newts, inedible coots and tadpoles that fascinated only their equals in the family of man. As the stream became too narrow, even for the canoe, I wanted to get out and wade on, as the boys must have done. But the moment I stood up the charm broke, for I was a giant looking out over a children's jungle, feeling foolish. So I sat down again facing the other way in the canoe, which, luckily, was not particular about stem or stern.

While I slowly poled my way back to my age, I felt a strange elation. It had to do with memories of my own boyhood, and with hopes for the future; it had to do with what I had felt the moment I penetrated into this small secret world of childhood, playing at explorer, perhaps for the last time in my life. I was indeed the first human being ever to penetrate into this magic garden, and so would the next boy be and the next, and the next, until finally the mangroves were uprooted by bulldozers, houses built on Oxford Circus, and the streamlet called the Thames. But, thank God, there were other virgin gardens still, and there always would be, even if the whole of the Florida jungle were to be subdivided into lots. For one wet summer, if hot enough, would turn any absent neighbor's garden into a virgin wilderness waiting breathlessly for its very first man, if young enough.

SHARKS' TEETH

THE BEACH near the town of Venice is sparsely sown with small black pebbles that, on close scrutiny, turn out to be black, triangular teeth.

They are prehistoric sharks' teeth that are estimated by local experts to be over a million years old and to have belonged to a ninety-foot sea monster called Carcharodon, which must have haunted this flat coast once—thousands upon thousands of sleek, tubular giants, thrashing in death. The sharks' teeth of Venice beach are one of the features of the town and quite often one sees elderly couples in long, wide shorts wandering further and further apart as they stoop arthritically to deposit another of Carcharodon's teeth in handkerchief or cooky tin, to add to their collection.

The sight of young couples spooning on the beach on a bed of sharks' teeth inspires the middle-aged stroller with philosophic thoughts. In this prehistoric land, so he reflects, the ribald song "Roll Me Over in the Clover" should read, "Roll Me Over on the Sharks' Teeth." Why, he asks himself, should this second version sound so sinister and the original so coarsely gay? For surely the clover is older in its eternal recurrence than Carcharodon, whose arid seeds now dot the shore. The young lovers on the beach are older still, carrying on as they do the spark of consciousness, blown into life by the breath of God, whereas Carcharodon is gone forever, and was gone forever a million years ago.

But all these golden thoughts are but the green leaves of youth turned autumnal; the distance between the young couples spooning on the sharks' teeth and the old ones stooping to collect them in their handkerchiefs is but a walk along a sunlit beach. In this country, where day and night are not measured by light and darkness but by periods of growth between the recurrent hurricanes, man with his threescore years and ten has but a couple of days to live, and the death throes of Carcharodon occurred last year.

So it all depends on how old the collector is, or thinks he is, when he picks up the sharks' teeth on Venice beach. In the small convex mirror of their black surface, scoured by the sand and polished by the sea, he sees, as in all mirrors, only his own ephemeral self.

DRIVE-IN SANCTUARY

In the days of the pioneers of the New American nation, prophets preached in the open underneath the trees. It must be this tradition that inspired the elders of congregations along the tourist routes of Florida to build "Drive-In Sanctuaries" where, underneath the whispering trees and the deep blue sky, earnest young preachers battle with the birds.

As St. Francis of Assisi knew, if one preaches in the open and the birds start to interfere, the only solution is to preach about them. This is probably what those early evangelists did as they stood in their hot, black clothes underneath a live oak tree and looked up at the exuberant little critters rustling and twittering in the foliage. To them they were not hecklers, but messengers from God, bringing them the sermon for that morning.

Not so in the drive-in sanctuaries of today. The faithful no longer arrive on horseback or in covered wagon, but by automobile. They no longer leave their means of transportation to gather around the preacher; they drive to small metal stands from which they pick up a loudspeaker without leaving their car. The preacher no longer stands underneath the trees, but is perched in a glass-walled signal box, soundproofed to keep out the sound of the birds, and his voice squawks the glad tidings through the loudspeakers hanging inside the automobiles.

The result is that the birds and the wind take over the sermon and that the glad tidings float overhead with the sailing clouds, while the electronic prophet in his signal box exhorts his congregation of unblinking head lamps not to fall into the trap of thinking that all creeds are good as long as they lead the soul to God. This, so the metallic little voice squeaks underneath the generous sky, is a fallacy. Only Our Church is certified to bring salvation; the others are, if not actually heathens, good-willing fellow travelers of Satan speaking with the voices of saints.

There is a small choir cooped up with the preacher in his signal box which sings the hymns the wind once swept away into the unconquered West; there is also a little electric organ, following the choir upon their heels. When the preacher's disembodied voice starts up again to finish off Buddha and Mohammed once and for all, one discovers the great blessing of the drive-in sanctuary: one can turn a switch.

In the sudden silence there are the birds, with their sermon.

THE RAIN FROGS
OF ROUTE 41

ONE night, as I drove along the highway between Sarasota and Fort Myers, Florida, in a tropical downpour I cursed, like my fellow motorists, under my breath as I was forced to slow down. I peered intently past the frantic wagging of the windshield wipers, blinded by the reflection of oncoming headlights; the rain turned into a deluge; then it was over, with the same violent suddenness with which it had begun. I gathered speed, and then suddenly I saw minute creatures in the beam of the headlights that seemed to sit up on the road, lifting small, powerless hands in a frantic plea for mercy before being crushed by the wheels of my juggernaut. There were hundreds, thousands of them, impossible to avoid; I was forced by the lights of the traffic behind me to ignore their tiny pleas and to lunge on through the darkness in a blind slaughter. In the end, the prayer of their pathetic little upthrust hands became so haunting that I risked a collision and swerved off the road.

My colleagues swished past, splashing me with the spray of their speed; when the last of them had vanished, a red glow of taillights in the darkness, I brought out a flashlight, shone it at the road and saw hundreds of small frogs, leaping across the road turned river with long, sinuous bounds, on a massive pilgrimage from darkness to darkness. As I stood there, looking at them, listening to the soft patter of their leaping, I heard other sounds in the night: a bird called from the reeds, cicadas chirped in the mangroves, and in the fast-flowing ditch alongside the highway fish leaped and splashed with joyful vitality. The realization dawned on me that these were the sounds of peace and contentment, that I only had to leave my car by the roadside out of mercy for the rain frogs of Route 41, to turn a corner of this dark and haunted trail and emerge in a wide-open space of joyful, timeless contemplation. But then there came, out of the night, the blinding beam, the roar, the swish and the drenching splash of a fellow driver in his machine, on the same dark pilgrimage from darkness to darkness as I, and I got back into the car. I started the engine, turned on the radio and while a choir sang, throbbingly, "April Love," I drove on with gathering speed toward my goal, trying not to heed the silent pleas of myriad little hands, stretched out beseechingly toward my blinding lights as they hurtled through the night.

THE SHRIMPERS

ONE summer evening I had to wait for the bridge
across the Caloosahatchee River at the village of La
Belle. From my car, I watched three shrimp boats from
North Carolina speed past with bravura, and reverse
into the small mooring basin just below the bridge.

The way the men handled their boats was a delight
to see, and I could not resist the temptation to get out
and watch them as they moored alongside each other in
the twilight. Below me, as I stood looking down on them
from the bridge, laughed and chatted the descendants of
the Apostles: three Negroes, two towheaded white men
and a Mexican. Nets were draped in the rigging as they
had been and still were on the River Jordan; from the
galley came the same smells that must have been wafted

across to the crowd ashore, waiting for miracles from Peter's pot. As I stood there, I saw a little man lower himself ashore from the innermost boat and climb the bank in the gathering dusk. It was the first time, I thought, I had seen a midget on board a ship; then, as he came toward me, I realized he was a little boy in man's clothes. He carried a sailcloth bag and approached me with the wariness of all small creatures approaching man. "Could you tell me where the store is?" he asked; I answered that it was across the bridge; if he liked, he could get into the car with me and I would take him there. He shook his head and said, "No, thanks. I'll walk." Obviously, I did not inspire confidence in the failing light.

I went on watching the three ships below, the gathering darkness and the reflection of the evening sky in the bend of the river. Then there sounded from the mangrove shrubs on the opposite bank the only song in the world that is better than that of a nightingale: the mockingbird's imitation of one. And from halfway across the bridge came an answer: a high, tremulous whistle, stringing out a hesitant little tune. The mockingbird caught it, touched it with its magic wand, and sent it back, luminous with joy and harmony. The whistler on the bridge tried another tune: the opening bars of "The Star-Spangled Banner"; the mockingbird, delighted, tossed it back as a string of jewels of sound. Then a voice called from one of the ships below: "Get a move on, Jake! Don't stand there whistling!" The boy and the bird fell silent.

I got into my car, switched on the headlights, and saw him walk away across the bridge, carrying his bag. Before I switched on the engine I heard the mockingbird call; it had almost forgotten "The Star-Spangled

Banner." The boy did not answer; he walked on as if he
had not heard. Then the mockingbird forgot him, and
took up its nightingale song, and I started the car and
drove past him, into the night.

A CEMETERY

ON THE banks of the river, between two villages miles apart, there is a small cemetery reached by a lane that crosses the fields. Cattle roam around it; armadillos scurry across the road, frightened by the footfall of the lonely visitor; silent vultures float overhead.

The graveyard is little more than a clearing in the swamp. Some old live oak trees stand among the graves, the rest is cabbage palm and jungle shrub. Outside the gate is a garbage pile of rotting flowers, withered wreaths and colored ribbons; among the cattle droppings in front of the gate lies a cardboard box: FASTEETH, KEEPS YOUR TEETH PERMANENTLY IN PLACE. On the aluminum gate itself is a plaque: LIFETIME GATES, INC.

The gate is secured with a piece of wire twisted around itself. It is quite an operation to disentangle it; obviously the latch was too easy for the cattle, eager for the grass among the tombstones. The tombstones give the cemetery an atmosphere of antiquity, for the sun and the rain of the tropics have done the work of three centuries in thirty years. Any inscription older than a decade can hardly be deciphered; the oldest among them, pink with age, sagging on one side, grown over with lichen, says SÖDERBLÖM—1925. Among the others, the only legible inscriptions left are on two small stones reading FATHER and MOTHER with two little hands clasped across the gulf of death. In the cemetery nothing seems permanent, not even the trees or the palms, only the neat metal plates at the foot of each grave, bearing the name of the funeral parlor, which have been calculated to withstand the harshness of the climate.

On one of the oldest stones, near the lifetime gate, is a cryptic legend: NOT HERE. No, indeed. Söderblöm never dreamed of being buried here, far from the fjords, the firs, the lakes glinting under the wintry sky. This is not home, not to the pioneer whose memory goes back to a childhood in the vineyards or among fishing nets silver in the sun, nor to any human being of our Western world. The only graves at home in these surroundings are the Indian mounds, where small boys find arrowheads and snakes bask in the sun on the oyster shells bleached by the rain and the wind. The heat, the cicadas, the huge yellow grasshoppers, the black thunderclouds on the horizon above the lake, the staring steers among the palmetto give a heartbreaking quality to the artificial forget-me-nots hanging in a little galvanized trumpet on the newest stone. A Negro spiritual seems to hum in the hot, still air. "Sometimes I feel like a motherless child, far away from home." But no Negroes are buried here. This godforsaken corner of the universe is for whites only.

The lifetime gate squeals shut; a hoof puts its print on Fasteeth; from the garbage pile three vultures rise, black witches screeching curses on the moors. The steers trot moronically into the swamp at the footfall of the lonely visitor trying not to flee.

DEVIL'S ELBOW

THE NAME, so they say, dates back to the time
when the hairpin bends in the Caloosahatchee River had
not yet been straightened by short cuts as they are now,
and this bend was one of the worst. The family living in
the white frame house underneath the giant live oaks on
the shore never went without oranges, for the wheezing
little steamer that came down the river from Lake
Okeechobee every week had to make such a sharp turn
in Devil's Elbow that at least four or five crates slithered
off the deckload each time, fell in the water and were
washed ashore among the hyacinths, the reeds and the
snakes.

Now the short cut has diverted the traffic, the steamer
that once came hissing round the bend has long since
been broken up, and the little boy who used to pick up
the oranges lived to be an old man, to whom his middle-
aged sons still refer fondly as "Daddy." Yet the frame

house has not changed much. The live oaks still overhang the water, draped with the giant gray cobwebs of the Spanish moss, and there still is a little boy messing around in the reeds and the hyacinths, whose mother's voice, calling from the house, reminds him of the snakes with a sound of exasperation.

It is the only sound in Devil's Elbow, apart from the full-throated bellow of an occasional towboat alerting Olga bridge, or the buzz of an outboard passing down the river, or the distant rumble of loose planks as a car drives across the bridge. To the weary traveler, resting awhile on the river's bank, it is a comforting thought that time has come to a stop in Devil's Elbow. Whatever may happen in the world at large, here there will always be a little boy messing about in the reeds and the hyacinths and the snakes, who have never within living memory done anybody any harm.

To talk to the little boy is to talk to the fullness of the present. He is unconscious of the passing seasons, he does not yearn for the future nor mourn the past, he is interested only in today and talks about it with earnest concentration. Do you know there is an old bull alligator in that patch of reeds over there, where the entrance to the bend used to be? You may think there is no path on the little wild island across the river, but there is, and he is the only one who knows it: a secret path, that comes out on the other side. The squirrels eat bread when his mother feeds them, but they will only take cookies from Miss Jones, the schoolteacher. And Paddlefoot the dog has had eight puppies; they are going to keep two of them and give the others away. Would you like a puppy? If you hurry you can still have first pick.

You would, but there is reality, waiting round the bend. If you were to stay in Devil's Elbow, and share the secret of youth with this old little boy . . .

But there blares a towboat, three roaring blasts, and there squeaks the old bridge as it turns to open, and the yearning that urges the wanderer on toward his unknown home spreads its silent, melancholy wings once more.

4 *The Everglades*

CONTENTS

A FRONTIER TOWN

To ENTER Clewiston harbor, on the southern
shore of Lake Okeechobee, in the gathering dusk of a
summer's night, is to feel for a moment like the captain
of a barque from Tarsus, entering Rhodes' majestic gate
in a starlit night of antiquity. The hurricane gates of
Clewiston are the most impressive entrance to any small
harbor I know; but once your ship, blaring its warning
between the reverberating walls that tower above you,
glides into the stillness of the basin beyond, it enters a
world dreamed of by James Barrie: a small harbor, lined
by romantic houseboats covered with little green frogs, a
dilapidated city dock where fireflies flit and a rabbit sits
patiently waiting for Peter Pan.

The only place to moor, for a ship of any size, is alongside a deserted barge of the Army Corps of Engineers,
tied up to trees at the edge of a lawn with a darkened
office building looming beyond it. The way to the town,
from there, leads through a cemetery. Its hazy headstones
and pale rings of recent wreaths are eerily lit by the
distant, quivering glare of electric signs: spinning wheels,

flashing arrows and dotted lines racing around the words "Motel," "Ice Cream" and "Broiled Burgers." The main highway from Palm Beach to the west coast runs straight through the town and at night it sounds like the Rhine in Rotterdam: trucks roar past like tugboats, buses swerve out of the current like ferries, to tie up to the Diner and disgorge a stream of passengers. The air has that familiar smell of fog, Diesel fumes and summer, and the raucousness of this landbound waterway is such that you need a few moments in which to adjust yourself to the brash vitality of this frontier town.

Across the road is a trailer park; a man, framed by a small lighted window, sits with his head in his hands, picture of dejection. Next door, a restaurant: four chimneys are smoking, dummies of cowboys and bad men lean over a rail on the roof, frozen in death spasms induced by past gales. Then a juke-box, in the open, at the hot-dog stand, bellowing "Lipstick on Your Collar" over the roar of the trucks. Next: CATERPILLAR DIESEL SALES: huge, esoteric monster tractors on stilts and airplane tires; a joker has attached a printed sign to one of them, GET ONE FOR YOUR WIFE! Next door, a funeral parlor, its Venetian blinds half-open, showing a small group of people praying at a bier. Then a dimly lit shop with, in its window, a notice: FLOWERS FOR THE LOVE LORN. A drugstore, a supermarket, and then the flashing, rippling and twitching electric signs of a long string of motels, diminishing in the distance. To the north, there is the big, ghostly lake; to the south, the immense wastes of the Everglades; to the west, the Atlantic, sixty miles away; and to the east, eighty miles away, the Gulf of Mexico. The town of Clewiston might as well be in the Arizona Territory, a century ago, or on the slopes of Mount Kepler on the moon, a century from now.

The restaurant is plastered with folksy humor. A big

notice over the gate says ENTERANCE and from there on
the customer is plied with jokes hanging in the windows,
nailed on the walls, painted underfoot. SAVE YORE
CONFEDERATE MONEY; FREE ASPERIN, KIND FEELIN'S AND
COOL, COOL WATER; COME IN, Y'ALL, THE BACK WAY and
finally WELCOME PARDNER, YORE IN FOR ONE ROLLICKING
TIME. The door opens with the lunatic sound of a cow-
bell; inside, a row of silent, exhausted truck drivers sit
slumped at a counter. Not a word, not a smile from one
of them; the waitress is exhausted also; the notices on the
wall—BUFFLER STAKES, EAT LIKE HELEN B. HAPPY—are
solitarily splitting their sides.

There is a smell of skunk in the darkness when you go
back toward the graveyard. Once the juke-box, howling "You're nothin' but a hound-dog," is left behind, the
crickets take over. The roar of the trucks subsides, and
your last glimpse of the town is the man in the window
in the trailer park, sitting with his head in his hands, a
picture of dejection, before you are safely back in the
world of James Barrie, beyond the graves.

OLD BROWN'S TRADING POST

THE GREAT wilderness of water, saw grass and clouds called the Everglades is one of the last really wild territories in the United States. The only way to penetrate into its heart is in a cumbersome vehicle called a swamp buggy, which is usually constructed by its owner. The buggy in which my American friend and I set out on our expedition to explore the sea of grass had been built by our guide. It was an old Ford Model A on airplane tires, with snow chains to grip the mud, and perched on top of this contraption, lurching and swaying as on an elephant, we bounced down the new road toward the wilderness on the first day of our journey. The Seminole Indian workmen building the road looked incongruous in the American laborer's uniform of khaki pants and khaki shirt; they were led by a red-faced white supervisor who was very hot. Two Indians lurched about on a couple of gigantic snorting bulldozers, painted yellow, that pushed carloads of sand in front of them into the marsh for the continuation of the road. There was sand everywhere along the track and broken young trees and lethal coils of rusty old barbed wire, last remnants of forgotten claims, now uprooted by the proud

Indians on their mechanical monsters.

"We'll stop here," our guide said. "I want to show you the monument." My friend asked, "Monument?" and the guide told us that this was the spot where Old Brown's Trading Post had been, subject of countless ballads and campfire stories among the Indians and the trappers of the Everglades. It had been a true outpost of progress; here the Indians had brought their wares to barter for guns, alcohol and patent medicine. Here the first Bibles had been handed out to them free with their month's shopping, and from here the first missionary had set out into the jungle, never to return. Some people said the missionary had settled on a hammock in the heart of the marsh, forgetting about converting other people once he was faced, like Jacob, with God in the wilderness. Others said he had been killed by the Indians or escaped convicts, but our guide himself thought he had probably crossed the Everglades and come out at the other end without having met anybody and gone elsewhere on his search for souls. We were, so the guide said with an odd reverence for so matter-of-fact a man, standing on hallowed ground. Old Brown's Trading Post had dominated this gateway to the Everglades for over half a century; it had been burnt down and rebuilt, besieged and relieved; shots had rung out and hymns had been sung, and from the eucalyptus tree in the shade of which evangelists had healed the sick, many a man had been lynched by ranchers whose cattle had vanished in the wilderness. This had been part of the dawn of America, and it was fitting that a monument had been erected to mark the site.

We got down and looked around for the monument; there was nothing to be seen but the mangrove shrubs damaged by the bulldozers, the soggy sand of the new

road, the coils of old barbed wire and the Indians on their
machines, thrusting and rearing in their slow, proud
jousting match.

"What are you guys looking for?" the sweating foreman asked as he saw us rummage in the shrubs.

"A monument," my friend said, with an ingratiating
smile because the supervisor looked sorely tried.

"Monument?" he said. "You don't mean the bit of
stone with the disk on top?"

We said we didn't know. All we knew was that somewhere around there there should be a monument to Old
Brown's Trading Post.

"Old who?" the supervisor asked in an alarming effort to be jocular. Then our guide came back from the
shrubs with his machete, and he obviously made the same
impression on the supervisor that the supervisor had
made on us.

"Where is the monument, you lousy sand pusher?" he
asked, his machete feigning indifference.

"How would I know?" the supervisor replied, a
small helpless cog in the vast machine of bureaucracy.
"Nobody's told me anything about a monument. I did
find a bit of stone with a metal disk on top but . . ."

"That's it!" the guide said. "Where is it? If you have
knocked the thing over . . ."

"Hell, no," the supervisor cried. "I ain't knocked nothing over. It's right here. It . . ."

"Look out!" my friend cried, and just in time, for
the supervisor had almost thrown himself in front of
one of his bulldozers as he scurried across the road. He
darted aside, shook both fists at the Indian high above
him, who ignored him and swung his monster round
with power and pride.

"Here it is!" the supervisor's voice called across the
white sand. "Right here!" We waded toward him, and

found him hastily dusting something with his rolled-up shirt.

It was the lowest monument I have ever seen, a milestone with a brass disk riveted on top of it. In the disk had been hammered, with irregular letters, THIS IS THE SITE OF OLD BROWN'S FAMOUS TRADING POST WHERE . . . The next few lines were illegible because of a recent scratch made with a big instrument, and the last line ended with: . . . BLESS AMERICA.

While the guide and the supervisor had words, my friend photographed the monument before it became part of the new road into nowhere.

Only much later, in the heart of the wilderness, did I realize what the real monument had been: the white road being born, the Indians on their bulldozers, proudly pushing their way into the haunt of ghosts where their ancestors were waiting. If the monument of Old Brown's Trading Post had been too small to see, the real one had been too big for three little ants, scrambling across a sand dune in the heart of the river of grass.

TWO INDIANS

THE SEMINOLE INDIAN has two names: one for the white man and one for his tribe. When I met an old Indian called Billy Airboat, I became very conscious of this fact. The old man in a beaded skirt, who stopped sweeping his front yard to raise his expressionless eyes at me, could not, by any stretch of the white man's imagination, have been called Billy Airboat for the eighty-odd years of his life.

My friend, who had romanticized the unconquered Seminole Indian for a lifetime, asked whether Billy Airboat would agree to having his photograph taken. The old Indian did not open his mouth, so our guide said, "Sure." I discovered that during our visit to the Indians in their reservation we needed an interpreter to translate not their language, but their silence. In this case no translation was necessary; never in my life have I felt such implacable contempt directed at me as when Billy Airboat looked at my Adam's apple.

Next door to Billy Airboat lives a preacher called Pedro Astute, who is an experienced traveler. His hut, thatched and wall-less like all Seminole dwellings, stands in a junk yard strewn with the wrecks of old automobiles that seem to be the hallmark of all Indian reservations. A child's handcart sits in the yard with a hen in it, and as the guide calls "Preacher Pete!" the first to emerge from the shadows of his dwelling are a couple of ducks. Then out he comes, small and leathery, in white man's trousers, white man's shirt, with a white man's haircut and the white man's pride when he says, "Last time I went there, I brought fifteen souls to God." The guide explains that "there" stands for another Indian Reservation and "God" for the Southern Baptist Church. My friend asks whether Mr. Astute would mind having his picture taken and the preacher says, "Go ahead, brother, by all means." When he takes up the motion-less stance of last century's football player, the hen turns away. His eyes do not look at my Adam's apple but, eagerly, at my heart. His rapture gives perspective to the depth of Billy Airboat's contempt, and his jeans show his old neighbor's skirt for what it is: the silence that no interpreter can translate.

BIG CYPRESS SWAMP

We had skirted the fringe of Big Cypress Swamp a week before penetrating into the Everglades. The friend with whom I made the expedition had taken me in his car from Route 41, the Tamiami Trail, to Immokalee, just to give me an idea of what the Everglades would be like.

The road was hot and dusty and quite new, with innumerable little bridges made of concrete, dazzling white in the sun. On the right-hand side was a ditch, and beyond that the Big Cypress Swamp.

It was just a forest of dead trees, draped with the torn shrouds of Spanish moss, and seemed endless. As we drove on, past mile after mile of dead, marshy forest dotted here and there with distant colonies of white birds that created the illusion of whitewashed cottages hidden in the woods, the Big Cypress Swamp began by its very monotony to exert a weird fascination. We began to understand why the legends of the Indians describe the big swamp as the home of ghosts and goblins, and why in their symbolic world the dead do not go on hunting in eternal pastures but, standing in slender canoes, silently drift among the pillars of the great and still cathedral that is Big Cypress Swamp. My friend and I, after driving silently along the new road alongside the great forest, both felt a longing to venture inside.

When we finally did, on top of our guide's swamp buggy that snorted and splashed its way pugnaciously through the Indians' Hereafter, it was quite different. There was no atmosphere of goblins and ghosts, nor did the Gothic caverns of the forest seem haunted by old men standing in slender canoes. The reason was, perhaps, that we followed a trail that had been bulldozed a year before by a crew of oil prospectors; if the forest was haunted by anything at all it was by the memory of that first exploration. On the hillocks between which the trail wove its way erratically, there were the remnants of those first white men's campfires: rusty cans riddled with the holes of pistol practice, beer bottles, and the broken bakelite casing of a portable radio set. At the sight of that shell inside which only a year ago had croaked multitongued voices in the stillness of the forest, it began to dawn on me why there was not a goblin left in the swamp. For what is the wandering glowworm of a will-o'-the-wisp compared to a shrill little voice singing, "Get regular the natural way!" to the accompaniment of a tambourine, from Tampa?

No ghost haunted by the memory of the living can silently glide nearer to God in the frail canoe of his dreams, if across the twilit path shimmering between the trees there crashes a yellow monster with a horizontal axe, thrusting its way toward man's eternal hope: oil. And the pistol shots, aimed at Libby's Pork and Beans for practice, must have chased not only the laughing bird, the owl and the roseate ibis, but also the pernicious jewel of Aloka, the giant spider in his web, and Treetah, the monkey, hiding human children he had stolen to teach his brood the way of men. And now here we were with our little machine, spluttering, splashing, lunging along the trail made by our big mechanical brother, and looking hopefully about us for the world of myth and mystery.

When, toward nightfall, we came splashing out of the forest into the boundless desert of water that was the Everglades, now blooming with the giant flower of the sunset, the guide said, "Well, that was Big Cypress Swamp. Did you fellows like it?"

We both hastened to say that we had liked it very much; neither of us confessed to our secret nostalgia for the Big Cypress Swamp as we had seen it from the outside that magic afternoon, long ago, last week.

THE EUNUCHS OF
THE WILDERNESS

To REACH the heart of the River of Grass you must pass through the outskirts of civilization.

Outside the last settlement of Immokalee there is a shanty town of the Negroes who work in the sugar fields; then the bleak barracks of the itinerant Mexican laborers; then the wall-less, thatched hovels of the Seminole Indians, brooding morosely among the rusty junk of broken cars. Finally, beyond the barbed wire of the outermost ranch, there is the great plain.

The last ripple of the concentric rings of man's civilization is the straggling herd of steers called scrub cattle, the lowest grade beef, roaming on the fringe of the wilderness. During the first day of your trek you still spot them occasionally, peering at the lunging swamp buggy from behind a palmetto shrub or a mangrove bush, with big pointed horns over eyes that are void of all comprehension. At first these steers, grazing in small bands on the shore of emptiness, are anonymous but as you venture deeper into the wilderness, the increasing loneliness turns them into individuals. Then there is the last straggler and the swamp buggy stops, impulsively, to hail the last living being before the void.

"You'll see they're quite tame," says the guide, who, the day before, had not even deigned to look at them as they fled, tails in the air, through the flooded pastures.

But the gazing steer is not tame. He is not wild either. He is just one mindless body of the great herd of castrated bulls, a eunuch in the wilderness.

The melancholy of this last steer before the great beyond is haunting. There he stands, knee-deep in the mire, staring at the big armadillo of the swamp buggy and its sun-hatted white mice with the vacant gaze of neuterdom. The birds, the wild cats, even the snakes that sparsely dot the waste of the Everglades all have an independence that suggests a personality, even from afar. When the limpkin swoops from the mahogany trees of a hammock and vanishes, squawking, in the waving grass, you feel that, if you could follow it and alight by its side and talk with it, you would hear fascinating tales of water, willows, toad and lizard, of eggs gleaming like ivory in the twilight and the tragedy of the lonely white feather floating on the lake. But no one on earth, not even the most humiliated and downtrodden, could ever talk with an Everglades steer. For here grows a body, and that is all; man has extinguished the spark of eternity within it, and with it, life itself.

As the swamp buggy splashes on into the wilderness on its lonely journey, you remain conscious of the steer gazing after you, even when you have lost sight of one another at last. There is in its gaze no sadness or reproach; it is the vacant gaze of irreparable idiocy, an imbecile in the death house. As the buggy splashes along, the dour guide suddenly starts to sing, the impulsive song of relief of all explorers as they finally face the great solitude where no one need wonder if he should be his brother's keeper.

THE BANYAN TREE

IN THE heart of the Everglades there is a small hammock called Hurricane Hill. At least, that is what the guide called it, but it may well have been "Hill 63A" on the government survey maps or "Moonshine Hammock" in the whisper of Betty's Bar in Immokalee. No one knows what the Calusas called it.

The Calusa Indians inhabited the camps in the Everglades long before the Seminoles; they were great mariners who are known to have sailed as far as the Leeward Islands in their canoes, and their disappearance is one of the mysteries of Florida. For of the Calusas there is nothing left, nothing at all, except some arrowheads, some broken pottery underneath the humus on little hills like this. My friend and our guide planned to dig a trench across, hoping to make a find.

As there was only one spade in the swamp buggy only one of us could dig at a time while another sifted the soil for treasures. The guide started to dig spadefuls of the rich black earth, while my friend, in a red checkered shirt, knelt by the side of the trench to sift the soil. They looked very young; as I strolled round the little hill, no bigger than a sand dune, I discovered that they fitted perfectly into the picture.

The little island was full of very young life. There were baby swamp rabbits with short ears, dumb with amazement at my appearance; there were flocks of young giant grasshoppers, brilliant red and yellow, learning to jump; there was a brood of scraggy gray young egrets that had yet to shed their baby down before emerging as the graceful white sprites of the wilderness. On the water's edge lay an enormous banyan tree, fallen on its side, which had gone on growing. Its air roots, tangled with the big round shield of its upturned ground roots, had created an intricate confusion of branch, limb and foliage, and the inside of this natural arbor was a veritable fortress of animal life. If I were a bird, I thought, this would be where I would want to spend my fledgling months, and if I were a young swamp rabbit this would be the place I would remember, while wandering bleakly through the wide, lonely world of water and wind.

As I slowly walked around the banyan tree and looked at the shield of its upturned roots, I saw something gleam in its confusion. At first I thought it was a piece of pottery, but as I looked more closely and bent some of the young roots aside I saw that it was the broken china head of a doll. Its colors had faded and it was quite white, but otherwise it had no age. It might have been there for a year or for half a century; now it seemed to belong right where it was: among the baby swamp rabbits, the young cardinals, the fledgling egrets, the grasshoppers going through their first earnest training.

But how had it got there, inside the roots of that banyan tree? It must have been put there before the tree fell. I stretched my hand out toward it, and then, as if I had turned a corner, I saw a dappled scene of sunlight and shadow, a little girl at the foot of a tree, solemnly burying a broken doll, her first funeral.

I dropped my hand, strolled back to the others, and squatted beside the trench, in which my friend and our guide were digging for the past with confident determination.

AN OLD WINDMILL

THERE are islands in the Everglades, few and far between, called hammocks, some of which are grave mounds of a prehistoric culture that existed long before the Calusa Indians or the Seminoles roamed these swamps, hunting bear and deer.

Yet, at first sight, the Everglades seem young. The grass remembers only the previous spring when it sprouted, green and eager, from the rustling corpses of last year's generation, and even that memory is hazy. For during the dry season, when no clouds sail through the steel-blue sky, the prairie makes its own: the brown, rolling clouds of the muck fire, when the dry grass bursts into flame by a mysterious spontaneous combustion. Regions as large as Manhattan are devastated by fire without anyone noticing or caring, only a brown haze on the horizon telling the lonely cowhand of the fury raging beyond the curve of the globe.

Even the grave mounds of the prehistoric Indians do

not give the Everglades any age. Man has, like the saw grass, sprouted from their withered leaves too long ago for them to be remembered as human. The flint arrowheads and axes strewn about those hills do not evoke an image of humanity; some chattering tribe of apes has gamboled here, imitating man by picking up from beach and quarry crude images of the older brother's tools. If the traces of these forgotten ancestors convey anything at all, it is a feeling of childhood; they make the Everglades seem even younger.

You can splash, grind, bump and slosh about with your swamp buggy in this desert of water and waving grass for days on end, spend night after night in jungle hammocks, suspended between palms on grave mound or hill, and still feel nothing but a sense of space, loneliness and a complete absence of the romance man needs to give perspective to the *décor* of nature. Then, after three days of aimless wandering in search of the soul of the wilderness, there it is, unexpected and with a suddenness that catches the breath.

Somewhere in the grass, among the clouds, the graves and the water, there is the gaunt, leaning structure of an iron windmill. It is old, as windmills go, at least fifty years, and it suddenly throws this ageless desert into perspective. Men have roamed here, driving their cattle before them; they have settled on these mounds, built camps, stables, houses; children have played in shady yards and women called through kitchen windows to their men in the sun at mealtimes. And then they disappeared, nameless as they had come, driven by the same urge that had made them emerge antlike from the round horizon, and all they left behind was this strange leaning tower with its squeaking weather vane and rattling wheel, rusted and gaunt. As the wind whispers in the saw grass, strokes the fur of this huge sleeping animal of weeds and water in Florida's heart, the wheel turns, squealing eerily in the silence, and the piston of a broken pump churns idly in its barren well. Fifty years, and not a trace left of house or barn, jetty or garden, nothing but this pointless structure pumping ghostly water from the swamp.

After seeing the dead windmill, you suddenly feel the urge to flee. You long for the swamp buggy to turn round and splash back to the new road at the border of the Indian reservation, to rumble into the silent Seminole village with its surreptitious lights. For only now have you recognized that village for what it is: an outpost of the present in the sea of man's past.

MOCCASIN HAMMOCK

IT IS one of the islands in the great River of Grass, three days' journey by swamp buggy from the southern boundary of the Seminole Reservation. It is no different from hundreds of its kind: a hillock with a campsite for those who wander through the wilderness to hunt or hide. It is, like all hammocks, clustered with palms and live oak, soggy in the wet season, and it smells of reptiles. The smell is a warning; when the waters of the wilderness rise, the snakes shelter on high ground, so the traveler who arrives at nightfall in Moccasin Hammock has no eyes for the eerie beauty of its setting in the copper of the sunset. All he has eyes for are snakes, as he gingerly lowers himself out of the buggy and cautiously treads his way through the sparse high grass toward the remnants of the last man's fire.

The guide, armed with a machete, disappears rustling in the dusk; from the echoing cavern of the little forest come the snapping sounds of dead wood and the dull thuds of the machete as a palmetto shrub is chopped bare to cut out its heart, the swamp cabbage.

Night falls quickly. One has barely strung up the jungle hammocks and lit the fire when darkness closes in. The great spangled dome of the night reduces the island to a molehill, and the little creatures round their glowworm fire to gnomes huddled under a cluster of fern on the brink of the great pond of darkness. Whenever a home-coming sailor says that nowhere in this world are the stars so big as in the Sahara or the Indian Ocean or the Everglades, what he really means is that there a great loneliness has made him feel small in the night. When the dying embers of the fire dim their glow and the three men, silent at last, lie gazing through the mosquito netting of their hammocks, the night closes in and with it the strange fear of the last great wastes of the earth.

It is not a fear of snakes or man. It has nothing to do with ghosts or anything else from the past. It has to do with man's loneliness underneath the biggest stars in the world, and man's breath in the great gentle wind that caresses the Everglades, the swamps, the ocean, space. To lie on his back in the night in Moccasin Hammock and to look up at the sky is as far as man dares venture into the interstellar void. No space rocket will ever be so isolated and alone as this little island, its palms, its snakes and the cricketlike snores of guide and friend in the great silence.

The cicada, so it is said, lives from four to twenty years as a nymph, blind and voiceless underground, finally to emerge and sing for one single week of summer. Man, when he finally emerges into space and is faced with the reality of his habitat, falls silent and longs dumbly for the dawn.

When dawn finally comes and sheds its comforting light, it reveals snakes, which are chased away, and traces of other fires built by other lonely travelers. There are rusty cans, old enameled pans of last century's cowpokes, the broken handle of an Indian earthenware jug and the flint almond of a Stone Age man's arrowhead. They are found with a feeling of relief and gratitude, for the arrow belonged to a brother, seen from the point in space to where the stars of Moccasin Hammock have enticed the beholder during this summer's night, which was almost the point of no return.

THE VULTURES

THERE are two kinds of vultures in the south of the United States: the black vulture which is actually black and gray, and the turkey vulture which has a pink, bald head. Both have a repulsive hopping gait before their take-off that suggests they have gorged themselves on carrion, even when they have not. The newcomer soon begins to share the loathing the natives feel for these birds that wheel forever in the sky. They are winged reminders of putrefaction, patiently waiting for the death of the foreshortened little men scurrying about below. Young boys shoot at bats, men shoot at vultures, and both feel equally impotent, even if they hit one.

There is only one place in the United States where the vulture reveals its true nature. After trekking across the great wilderness of the River of Grass for days man comes to long for their familiar silhouettes in the sky. For the silent watchers, spiraling overhead wherever he goes, vanish from the sky once the last straggler of the herd of scrub cattle has been left behind. On the second day the black kite of loathing slowly wheels away, and leaves the sky to the ibis, the egret, the anhinga and the limpkin, who have no relationship with the community of man.

The disappearance of the vulture from the sky brings about the illusion that in this timeless land of wind, grass and water, there is no death. But instead of feeling relieved and immortal, man feels haunted by a weird and unexpected fear. He realizes that the silent reminders of death in the sky are part of his life and the way he lives it. Even in their loathsomeness, the buzzards are part of his reality. Instead of feeling immortal in space now they are gone, he feels ghostlike, already dead, and, finally, ephemeral to the point of nonexistence.

There are, in the twilit world between insect and amoeba, little transitory creatures whose individual life is so pathetically short, in man's conception of time, that no name could possibly be allotted to them, as they do not even live long enough to outlast the utterance of it. Man in his little buggy, splashing underneath the empty sky in this roadless expanse of rippling grass and sparkling water, feels that whatever word God may have for immortality, he will not outlast its utterance. This is not I, who travel through space with him, my friend; we are not even we; we are a species, living and dying in a constant hum of massive death and resurrection in a twilit world between Gods and rocks, mind and matter, in a void sprinkled sparsely with the electrons of stars and the neutrons of their planets.

The crossing of the Styx of grass takes an eternity of four days and nights. On the morning of the fifth day, the guide points up and cries, "Look!" There, circling silently overhead, is the familiar black kite of the first vulture. It is no longer loathsome, it is a harbinger of the shores of reality, after this crossing of the ocean of space that for one second in eternity has determined our notion of time.

THE GUARDIANS OF THE GARDEN

IN A small town on the southern shore of Lake Okeechobee, there live in the eternal wind underneath the eternal pageant of the clouds the guardians of the wildlife refuge of Nicodemus Slough: a branch of the United States Army Corps of Engineers.

Poets and adolescents have frowned for generations at the insensitiveness of museum attendants and graveyard keepers; even Hamlet asked the nameless skull in his hand questions which had never occurred to the levelheaded little man busily digging behind his back. This is, of course, as it should be; the museum would be ransacked if the attendants stood in front of Mona Lisa, lost in her smile; and a gravedigger who, leaning on his spade, philosophized about the seasons of man would soon find himself in an almshouse or a pulpit. So it is just as well that the members of this branch of the Army Corps of Engineers do not go wandering about Nicodemus Slough sniffing at flowers, watching the white egret primping up to her knees in her mirror, or marveling at the diamond of a spider in its web of pearls in the roseate dawn. But as you cannot, being human and malleable in the hands of God, remain uncorrupted by the playful riot of nature after staying in the heart of this magic gar-

den for any length of time, the Corps flag outside the
office of the Corps of Engineers is hoisted upside down,
and the notice board in the hall, recording the whereabouts of the officers, shows the whole staff to be "In"
as well as "Out."

The office building is situated between the churchyard and the hurricane gates; a somnolent barge lies
growing grass on its deck at the buttercup-spangled
bank, and up the pillars of the porch crawl bright green
rain frogs, waiting for the night to fill the firefly-haunted
darkness with their trumpeting.

Our guide, with whom we were about to vanish into
the prehistoric garden of Nicodemus Slough, had an errand in the building with a good friend of his. He
frowned as he narrowed his eyes to read the list of names
on the wall, then shrugged and wandered off in
search of his friend, leaving us behind in the hall. We
looked at the maps of the levees of the district, the water
levels of the lake, the yellowed interoffice communications pinned on a cork board, and caught a glimpse of
the great silver lake through the crack of a door marked
PRIVATE. After a while my friend, who had disapproved
of the empty silence, the confusion about the officers'
whereabouts and the flag, began to fall under the spell.
It seemed as if there were nobody here to do anything
at all; yet there were the great levees, the hurricane
gates, the well-kept lawn, the well-painted flagpole. As
his viewpoint slowly drifted upward toward divine ob-
jectivity, he remarked how well the pole was painted
and forgot about the flag. We had been wrong to think
of the invisible men, both "In" and "Out," as museum
attendants or cemetery wardens. We discovered as we
sat in that hall and listened to the silence that they were
the Gardeners of Eden.

When our guide came back, we asked him whether he had found his friend and he said no, he didn't seem to be in this morning. But never mind, he had since realized that his errand could wait.

NICODEMUS SLOUGH

FEW people ever go to the wildlife refuge of Nicodemus Slough, for the road of access leads along the big levee which is under the control of the Corps of Engineers, barred by two padlocked gates, and once you reach the refuge proper you can proceed only by swamp buggy.

The moment the guide has unlocked the gate to the levee and driven the buggy through, you feel you have entered a magic world. The highway is only a few yards behind, yet you are already miles away from the cars swishing past on the asphalt. Here, in the warm lee of the windbreak of pine trees and bamboo, the small nomads of the animal world mill about like squatters outside the walls of the great cities of antiquity. When the wildlife refuge was instigated twenty-five years ago, its purpose was certainly not to preserve the precious frog, the exquisite possum or the rare raccoon; but the fact that neither guns nor dogs are allowed on the levee has created a small-animals' wonderland. In order to know what difference it makes to the living creatures of this earth to be liberated from the menace of man, you have only to stroll slowly along the top of Moore Haven's levee toward the refuge of Nicodemus Slough and listen to them croak, warble, quack and trill their psalms of praise.

Once you have passed through the second gate, and the chains have been hitched onto the buggy's wheels and the clumsy contraption paddles into the sanctuary of Nicodemus Slough, the animals get bigger. There are the scrub cattle, descendants from the herds of the first Spanish settlers, safe from rustlers now they have wandered into the refuge; there are the fugitive farm hogs turned native, gamboling and frolicking with their chestnut-colored brood in the shady arbors of the hammocks; there are the thousands and thousands of birds: egrets, ibises, cranes, water turkeys, limpkins, herons, eagles, hawks—not just occasional flocks of them, but tribes, whole nations, taking to the air at the noisy approach of the buggy like a snowdrift swirled up by a storm. The small cypress swamps echo with the garrulous monologues of crows and the melancholy hoot of the bittern; and among the irises, the lilies and the pickerelweed on the fringes of the swamps there scurry the little moor hens, black and white, whole nunneries of them, walking the water.

Yet the heart of Nicodemus Slough is still a long ride away, protected by gullies and marshes, treacherous swamps into which the buggy sinks up to its hubcaps, and an impenetrable wall of thorny shrubs. There is an entrance and the guide knows it, but he has to stop the buggy and investigate on foot, wading out into the lake of a crossroads to discover whether the rut has not been worn too deep by the swiftly flowing stream since his last visit.

Those few moments, when his passengers sit waiting silently on top of the buggy as he wades out into the open, are full of wonder. In the silence after the buggy's engine is switched off the myriad sounds of Paradise hum, buzz and zoom around the intruders. Around the half-submerged guide fish leap and splash defiantly. Overhead, between the branches of two small cypress trees timidly leaning toward one another across the stream, a spider has woven its web; as the sunlight strikes the dewdrops on it and turns it into a pirate's treasure, you know that if only you could stay long enough to forget about yourself, you could write the love poem of the two young trees and the swashbuckling story of the spider in his jeweled lair.

Then the guide comes wading back, and my friend asks, "What are those fish jumping for? Are they being hunted, or is it for their digestion?" The guide, as he hoists himself, dripping, back behind the wheel, shrugs his shoulders and answers, "Dunno. Here they just jump for the heck of it."

He starts the engine again, and the conceited little buggy steams on, while the fish jump for the heck of it, the trees have eyes only for one another, the moor hens walk the water oblivious of the miracle and the crows, after a reckless coot has asked them how they are today, go on telling him until the sun sets at the end of a wonderful day.

THE ROSE OF BITTERSWEET HAMMOCK

In the heart of Nicodemus Slough there is a small shady hammock where we stop to have a meal. The buggy climbs ashore, after having lived for half an hour as a boat; among the trees of the hammock scrub cattle start to flee, but then fall victim to their curiosity and stop to gaze at the intruders from behind palm trees where they imagine they are invisible. A meal on Bittersweet Hammock is not for the squeamish, for the ground is covered with cow dung and the guide scoops the water for the coffee from the swamp. As guns are not allowed inside the refuge, you cannot, while waiting for the guide's concoction, chase the staring cows or your encroaching uneasiness by pistol practice on a beer can; all you can do is wander about the hammock, gingerly because of the snakes, and taste an orange of the tree that stands in the middle of a clearing. "Yes," the guide calls, "Taste one! They're still sweet."

So they are. The tree must have been planted no more than thirty years ago, or it would have gone bitter by now. Sucking an orange, you look around you; you can still see the vague outline of the settlement that must have been here. The orange tree is the last of a small grove, the clearing with its balding saw grass must once have been a lawn, and underneath the old live oak, un-kempt with dangling moss, there must have been a cabin, secure underneath the giant boughs of the tree that would remember the early Spaniards if it could be bothered. And as your eyes wander along the edge of the scrub, where the cattle are still peering in their stub-born quest for understanding, you suddenly see the heart of Nicodemus Slough.

It is a small, secretive bush with one small touch of color which looks like a butterfly until, after your cau-tious approach, you discover it to be a yellow rose.

You stand looking at that rose, the half-eaten orange in your hand, and feel as if you were about to lift the veil of the past. If only you could stand there a little longer, you would know who it was that had lived here, built that house, planted that tree, sown that lawn, to add, one budding morning in a forgotten spring, that rose as a symbol of his happiness.

But then the guide calls, "Come and get it!" The cattle turn and rustle away in the scrub; all the rosebush has revealed to you in your stubborn quest for understand-ing, is that happiness.

THE GREAT AMERICAN BIRD

THE PILGRIM FATHERS hunted the wild turkey, ate it and gave thanks; it was the beginning of a great joy for the new nation and of a great sorrow for the turkey. In the centuries that followed, as the American population began to number millions, millions of turkeys were raised for slaughter at Thanksgiving and Christmas, and so there is now no American alive who can see a turkey without instantly thinking of roasting it. I can furnish no better measure of the Paradisiacal state of Nicodemus Slough than that here the wild turkeys are not afraid of man.

We came across a flock of them somewhere in this vast, wild garden, and the guide instantly swerved the swamp buggy off its course to pursue them. He had no intention of shooting them; it was just an instinctive reaction. At the other birds we had seen he had only pointed, crying, "Look, a Mexican Eagle!" or "There goes a wood ibis!" but at the sight of the turkey the force of tradition made him splash and bump after the fleet animals that barely increased the speed of their graceful gait to keep their distance.

Watching the wild turkeys turn flight into dignified disapproval was to understand their sad and pensive brother in its cage, waiting for the birthday of man's Savior. It must have in its wordless mind this very image: a flock of its gray muscular brothers, running sedately through water and marsh, pursued by a panting, swaying, snorting monster, ridiculous in its powerless greed. The guide stood up behind the wheel and shouted, "Bang!" and "Ratatat!" but these sounds meant as little to the unhurried birds as the cry of "Radiation!" would mean to a Papuan. So he stopped the buggy, got out some bread from under the seat, broke off a piece and threw it at the turkeys. This was the moment at which, of one mind, they took to the air.

That night, round the campfire, we talked about the sanctuary of Nicodemus Slough, and how we seemed to have wandered into Paradise. Both the guide and my friend agreed that the American idea of Paradise was best expressed in the painting of the old Quaker, Edward Hicks, "The Peaceable Kingdom" which is the New World's version of the Garden of Eden. It is a primitive painting, showing guileless children playing with a mixed company of panthers, lambs, mountain lions, doves and fox cubs. In the background is the great Quaker, William Penn, concluding his peace treaty with the Indians. The only thing lacking, so my companions agreed, in that picture of the American Paradise was a long festive table decked with flowers and fruit, bread, all kinds of cheese and cold turkey.

So, even after the peaceable kingdom has materialized, if you see a turkey gazing morosely at the horizon through the bars of its pen, from which it could flee if only it knew whither, sidle up to it, look to the left, look to the right, and whisper, "Everglades."

THE LOVELY SCOURGE
OF THE SOUTH

IF YOU ask the bargees or the tugboat captains to name the scourge of the South, they will answer without hesitation: the water hyacinth. And you cannot help reflecting what a blessed country this is, that even its scourge should be so ravishingly beautiful.

The water hyacinth, so those who have studied the question tell us, was introduced into the United States in the latter half of the last century by a lady who loved gardening and who was presented with a basket of blooms for her pond by a nameless beau in Brazil. She put the small posy of his adoration tenderly in her pond and let it float out of her white hands into the sky; it drifted silently away, among the clouds and the lily pads, and proceeded to choke the rivers of the South with its silent message of love. If ever there was a romantic flower it surely is the water hyacinth, and no throttled life lines of any other country can boast a sweeter strangulation.

The bloom that floated from the lady's hands multiplied a zillionfold and now the bayous of Louisiana look like meadows, the lakes of Florida flower with delicate mauve blossoms and even in that hidden fairyland of solitude, Nicodemus Slough, the blooms of love drift down Fish-Eating Creek by the thousands. The only thing that gives away the sad truth that they are not flowers but weeds is the fact that they have no scent.

The traveler, seated on the banks of this romantic stream, gazing at the silent procession of posies, bouquets, flower beds and triumphant islands of blooms, becomes aware that the water hyacinth's disastrous invasion of the waterways of the South is a quest for an elusive goal. To sit on a river's bank and watch the hyacinths float by, accompanied by their reflection, first inspires the beholder with philosophic thoughts, then with silence, and in the end with an inexpressible feeling of hope. For whether the hyacinth ever reaches the bliss of scent or whether the traveler will ever behold the dawn of truth, seems, after this glimpse of eternity, immaterial. What counts is hope itself; rare and precious are the moments when this silent message comes floating down the stream of life.

INDIAN PRAIRIE

THE FIRST time I set eyes on Indian Prairie was from the banks of Fish-Eating Creek. There, across the still water in which the hyacinths drifted among the clouds, I saw a silver world, guarded by motionless ibises and a host of snowy egrets. The boundless waste of water, saw grass, sky and clouds radiated an exultant promise; the promise of journey's end, the goal of all forgotten pilgrims. I asked the guide what it was and he said, "That's Indian Prairie."

I stood gazing at the promised land, trying to put into words what it was that held this great promise, what the secret was of this dazzling radiance of peace and hope. But I turned away without the answer; all I had acquired was the haunting knowledge that, somewhere in the heart of this continent of mountains and rivers, of thundering cataracts and chortling brooks, there was a place called Indian Prairie where the Indian warriors had gone to their eternal bliss and where there was peace.

The next day we penetrated, again by swamp buggy, into a forest of fallen palm trees, tangled vines and dead cypress draped with moss. After a struggle of hours the forest suddenly broke open into a great expanse of light and water. As far as the eye could reach there was a silver desert of water and grass, and again this land of promise was guarded by the motionless sentinels of ibises, perched on their watchtowers of oak across the river, and again, in the far distance, there was the fluttering white flock of thousands upon thousands of dancing egrets. The peace we faced across the still water stunned us to silence; after we had stood watching for a long time, overawed by its eerie bliss, my friend asked the guide, "Indian Prairie again?" and the guide nodded.

"Let's go there," I suggested.

But the guide shook his head. "Too far for us," he said.

I have since seen Indian Prairie many times. I have seen it open up beyond small towns, at the turning of a highway, behind a fringe of palms on the coastline, at the far end of the canyons of Manhattan. It is the soul of America that the white man will forever hope to capture, it is the reason why the keynote of the American dream is conquest, and the core of the American doubt a sense of futility. Indian Prairie is everywhere on this continent, yet no white man will ever get there. It is too far for us.

5 The Atlantic Seaboard, South

CONTENTS

A LAKE

LAKE OKEECHOBEE is a luminescent limbo between two worlds. To the west, there is the Caloosahatchee River, lined with old steamboat docks, petrified dinosaur bones and jungle hammocks, leading to the dignified, palm-pillared city of Fort Myers and, eventually, the Gulf of Mexico. To the east, there is the St. Lucie Canal, St. Lucie River and, beyond that, the part of Florida that is called the Gold Coast: Palm Beach, Miami, Fort Lauderdale, all of them washed fruitlessly by the Atlantic Ocean.

To enter Lake Okeechobee from the west is to enter the most magnificent avenue of trees in the world. It is the "rim route," a canal that came into being as the big levee was built around the lake, after the hurricane of 1928 which killed nearly two thousand people. At the time of its construction, trees were planted by the Army Corps of Engineers at the foot of the levee and on the spill bank across the canal, Australian pine interspersed with bamboo. This was thirty years ago; what at the time was a sensible device to prevent erosion has been turned by nature into a breath-taking Roman Road, small remnants of which may be found in Tuscany and the French Provence.

The section of the rim route usually taken by ships crossing the lake stops at the medieval rampart of the hurricane gate at Clewiston; from there, the most direct route to the east is straight across the lake: a boundless expanse of hazy, luminous water underneath a sky that is never without clouds. Beyond the horizon, in the un-inhabitated wastes of the Everglades, mysterious peat fires are perpetually smoldering, producing sudden, menacing palls of smoke that rise above the horizon like thunderclouds and are taken by the uninitiated to be storms brewing.

When you set out to cross it in your ship, the lake makes you feel small at first as you venture into its world-large, pearly shell; then, as you lose sight of the shore, the skyline behind you turns a translucent, milky blue underneath the black thunderclouds of smoke, resting on the pyramids of their reflections. Disembodied water hyacinths, floating in space, throw a spell that plays havoc with your sense of proportion. Suddenly you feel like a seafarer in a legend, Indian Ulysses sailing his barque among an archipelago of mangrove islands, which no man has ever set eyes on. Then the sunset sets the sky aflame, the mist on the horizon turns a fiery red, the shore seems to be blazing with a raging brush fire; darkness, as it slowly descends, brings the fleeting feeling, dreamlike, that a civilization has been here, unremembered by man, wiped out by hurricanes.

The awesome night takes over and the ship glides on, ghost vessel trailing shrouds of fog, headed for the timid twinkle of Port Mayaca's outer beacon, flashing in the void. You switch on the radio direction finder, to take a bearing on Belle Glade Station, and suddenly the silence

is torn by a quartet of nasal male voices singing hill-
billy songs in a high falsetto, caterwauling about "lur-
hurve," sounding as alien and unerotic as Chinese trouba-
dours. "Special from Belle Glade's News Room" comes
yesterday's news, interspersed with commercials: "Do
you lie awake nights, worrying about disease? Well,
here's your answer: whether you grow watermelons,
peppers or tomatoes, Dinosol All-Purpose Spray will
keep them healthy." A market report follows, recited
in a Gregorian chant by a woman announcer; at that
hour, on that lake, in that Stygian night, she sounds like
the priestess of a cult of virgins in antiquity. Columbus,
approaching the dark shores of the New World, cannot
have felt more alien than the mariner approaching Port
Mayaca at dawn.

On the small outlying islands of the eastern shore nest
the birds of the night; they rise screeching, gawking,
flapping huge wings, as your vessel passes on her way toward the bridge at the entrance of the St. Lucie Canal.
The bridge, after long, repeated wails of the ship's siren,
is opened by a man with dangling suspenders, cursing the
youthful lack of foresight that once put him there.

And there, ahead of you, stretches the canal, dead
straight, deserted, with a fierce current, leading to a last
romantic vision of south Florida before civilization takes
over: the St. Lucie River. Alligators, mangroves, families of turtles on fallen palms; after the lake this spells
home, even to a man from the North, for a night on
Lake Okeechobee is a night with the gods.

A COVE

On the fringe of Florida's Gold Coast, amidst the riches of palatial homes and expensive powerboats, under the banshee screams of the Miami radio stations, lies a small landlocked harbor called Manatee Pocket.

The dock belongs to a trailer park called Pirate's Cove, and nothing could be less aptly named. The little park is the very image of unaggressive tolerance, dominated as it is by pelicans, one to a piling, who sit waiting on the dock for the elderly anglers to return. They terrorize them out of their meager catch by flapping their wings, shaking their floppy beaks at them with an ominous gobble, barring their way with barrel-chested pugnacity until the intimidated oldster, cooing baby talk, has forked out his last minnow and turned his bucket upside down.

Pirate's Cove is a refuge from the aggressiveness of the Gold Coast. Its inhabitants, in all their elderly frailty and eggshell-delicate defenselessness, seem hardier than the fat men with foam-rubber caps driving their rearing powerboats to the slaughter of inedible fish in the Gulf Stream. The trailers stand in tiny gardens surrounded by miniature fences; most of them are put up on concrete blocks and have their wheels removed. At the miniature gates are name plates saying THE KRUGERS or THE JOHN-STONES. There is an atmosphere of happiness and quiet, almost mischievous gaiety about, despite the fact that a notice board at the entrance of the park says sternly ADULTS ONLY—NO PETS.

In the evening, strolling along the narrow lanes in the gathering dusk, you see lights go on in the trailers, and all around you small images of tenderness spring to life. Old ladies stand over stoves that have lost all suggestion of slavery and turned back into the dolls' stove and the first Christmas' toy dinner set; husbands sit reading the newspaper at arm's length or with close, magnified scrutiny. A gramophone plays, discreetly, "The Merry Widow Waltz"; in the manager's house an electric organ with full tremolo quavers its way through "To a Wild Rose."

Somewhere on board a visiting powerboat tied up at the dock, a radio is turned on, full blast, to the Miami Marine Operator forecasting "sce-attered she-owers" followed by the crackling monologue of an unbelieving wife, asking, "Haven't you caught enough yet?" and "Why don't you come home *now?*" interspersed with electronic blips, as her husband is lying on another wave length. At the first thud of a squirrel leaping onto the roof of a trailer, you will be startled, but you soon get used to them; when you finally stroll back to the dock, you will look round, expecting to be followed by an ankle-high crowd. But the squirrels remain behind among the senior citizens; they do not encroach upon the territory of the pelicans, who will eye you with one baleful golden eye to decide if you are worth frisking. On the powerboat, as you pass, ice tinkles in a glass and a voice says, "Isn't it gloomy here! Couldn't you have found something a bit livelier, honey?"

When I came back to the ship, my two dogs, small silhouettes with expectant ears against the evening sky, wanted to go ashore, and I set them free. There was a five-alarm scramble among the pelicans, two of which crash-landed during take-off; when the two excited mutts hit Pirate's Cove Trailer Park, they caused a wave of telltale barks and meows from the Krugers in the north to the Johnstones in the south.

It seemed typical of the place that the manager chose that moment to start playing "Jerusalem" with both feet down and all stops out, drowning out the sound of sin with militant Christian charity.

A POST OFFICE

THE POST OFFICE is a small, whitewashed building with screens in its door and in its two little windows. It stands in the shade of an old leaning tree, the kind of gnarled, tortured tree you find only at the seaside, and it overlooks the ocean. A dusty dog lies stretched out full length in front of the door, asleep.

The post office must have stood there for many years, catering a few hours each day to the needs of the few inhabitants of this inhospitable spit of land, which consists of nothing but sand, helm grass and a few old trees, like the one that shades the post office, their backs to the prevailing wind. But the days of the post office are numbered, for around it there has sprung up from the sand a mirage of the future, a city of stainless steel and glazed tiles, dazzling in the sun; behind the buildings stand the spidery turrets and the slender silver columns of the great ships, about to soar into interstellar space. This is Cape Canaveral.

Visitors are not allowed on the base, but the towers and the rockets are so gigantic that you see them glistening from afar, and what you cannot see is supplied in effigies by the diners, the motels and the donut shoppes, called space-age names like "Satellite Bar," "Minute-

Man Snackhouse" and "Sea Missile Motel"; most carry plaster mock-ups of rockets and satellites on their roofs or their façades. There is a lot of traffic of laboratory workers, the military and tourists, and the road has suffered accordingly. A high ambulance with a red cross painted on it sways and staggers among the potholes; a cradlelike Cadillac from Montana bounces like jelly among the snarling M.G.'s and Austin-Healeys of the locals. Around the old towns and villages across the Indian River, places like Titusville, Cocoa and Melbourne, whole new suburbs of identical bungalows have sprung up to house the families of the rocketeers; supermarkets, drugstores and department stores are mushrooming along the highway. The atmosphere of the place is unique and a little awesome; this is, with its unknown Russian counterpart, man's steppingstone into space.

It is comforting to see the wives, their heads in curlers, shopping lists in hand, stand as earnestly in front of a display of baby foods in the supermarket as their husbands stand in front of their blackboards covered with hieroglyphics. The idea of baby foods piled up on the brink of space gives comfort to Old World eggheads, who wonder whether man's mechanical ingenuity combined with his moral imbecility is not going to make this planet the biggest rocket of them all. The only power between us and our annihilation seems to be the earnest young mothers, weighing the respective merits of strained prunes and strained turkey-and-rice baby dinner.

So I say to the visitor from abroad: if you want despair, go and gaze at the men and their hardware; if you want hope, go to the supermarket, where you may put a dime in a mechanical rocking horse to keep the future of mankind quiet a few minutes longer, while its mother mans the breach.

"IF YOU WON'T
COME TO CHURCH . . ."

EDUCATIONAL experts have already warned you, but let me warn you again: be careful with threats you might use on a child to have it do your bidding. They will sink into his subconsciousness and are sure to emerge from that moonlit lake in the adult's dreams, to terrify the wits out of him at the most unexpected moments.

When I was a small boy my stern Dutch Reformed aunt Minna took a grim view of the way I tried, every blessed Sunday the Lord gave, to wangle my way out of going to church with her. My excuses were varied and many, and as she was not a woman beflown by poetic imagery, her threats were elementary. First she said I would not get any supper unless I went, which has made me hungry in church ever since. When the specter of hunger as a punishment proved no longer effective, she let out the admonition which, forty years later, wreaked its revenge when I stood at the wheel of Rival, sailing up the Indian River. To the rebellious boy, my aunt, a black statue of wrath with chalk-white hands and face, had cried, "If you won't come to Church, one day the Church will come for you!" I cannot describe my primeval terror when, that peaceful sunlit afternoon on the Indian River, I saw a church coming for me.

In this land of the unexpected, the traveler is subconsciously armed for any surprises, but to see a church afloat, pulled by a little tug, seemed a hallucination. There it came, complete with vestry, Gothic windows and a cross on its gable, perched precariously on top of a rusty barge called Belcher. The tow was slow, so was Rival, so we passed one another sedately. The helmsman of the tugboat gaped at the Dutch galleon bearing down on him with bulging sails, the helmsman of the galleon gaped at the church. When were abeam of one another, we both cried at the same time, "Where're you going?" I answered, "Holland, via Nantucket Island!" which seemed sane enough to me. He replied, "Satellite Beach!" which, I suppose, seemed sane enough to him.

If I could have described to my aunt Minna what I saw that afternoon, a floating church on its way to Satellite Beach, I know how she would have reacted. When I booked my first literary success, she said somberly: "Good thing I'll soon be leaving this vale of tears, for I surely don't know what the world is coming to. When you were a child you were punished for your lies, now you are paid for them."

She would not have believed a word about satellites, rockets, television, atomic bombs. She would not have believed that there is a country on this earth where whole churches, ready-made, are loaded onto barges and sailed hundreds of miles across open water to be let down on a beach as barren as a reef. I found out later, from the newspaper, that it was a secondhand church, picked up somewhere cheap, and I knew then that the only thing my aunt would have believed about Cape Canaveral was that, outside the pale of this dazzling city of glass and chrome, where thousands of people spend millions of dollars to explore the heavens, a secondhand church with a sagging porch and lopsided Gothic windows sits patiently waiting for those who, having explored the heavens, have found no answer to the immortal longings that have haunted man ever since he lit his first fire on earth, and that will go on haunting him until he has lit his last.

A LAGOON

NORTH of Cape Canaveral, Indian River draws to
a close and leads to a unique and eerie world. The town
of Titusville is the last stop before the pleistocene
world of Mosquito Lagoon.

Titusville has been drawn into the orbit of the missile-
launching base only as far as its landward side is concerned; the launching of the satellites has not yet changed
its waterfront. There is a staid, highly respected boatyard where speedboats are still built as they were in the
thirties, called "Correct Craft"; there is a pleasant marina,
but the entrance to the harbor is tricky; the channel between the pierheads, indicated by a red buoy, has narrowed to a point where it is virtually closed. Those who
squeeze in, however, will find a pleasant haven in what
turns out to be a tidal basin between two worlds.

At night, there may be a sudden fiery glow in the sky,
the distant roar of a mythological dragon, and an orange
halo will slowly rise towards the stars; but it does not
interrupt the persistent parlando of a harmonica from
the single lighted window of Correct Craft, nor stop the
restless seagulls preening their feathers on the pilings. All
through the night, the melancholy hoots of Diesel loco-
motives bawl plaintively at the level crossing, pulling

trainloads of top-secret parts to Cape Canaveral, but on the waterfront all is peace.

The transition from Indian River to that other world begins the next morning at dawn. The ship cautiously noses out of the harbor and sets course for Haulover Canal, the entrance to Mosquito Lagoon. The approach channel to Haulover Canal has been dredged through sandy shallows, and its spill bank has created a string of small islands on which flocks of white pelicans squeeze closer and closer together as their land gets smaller with the rising tide. All of them take off when an eagle, alone on one of the islands, rises majestically into the air.

It is sunrise. The air is limpid, the water an incredible blue. At the far end of the channel lies the double image of the dark trees bordering the canal. A bridge crosses the canal, halfway to the lagoon; the man who slowly opens it turns out to be the gatekeeper of a timeless world as you emerge into the glassy silence of the lagoon.

Disembodied little fishing boats float high above the hazy horizon. Fishing birds are bobbing on the mirror of the water by the thousand, separated from their reflections by a silver band. To the west, where the channel follows the shore, dead trees stand crown-deep in the water, covered with black cormorants like ravens, drying their wings. The black birds and the streaks of their excrement, stark white, that cover all tree stumps, logs and foliage, give the western shore of the lagoon an atmosphere of starkness, as if it were painted in black and white. The brevity of individual life, observed as you slowly float past, becomes haunting: all around you, birds catch fish; what is one moment a silver marvel of God's artistry is swallowed in a choking, greedy gobble and squirted out a few hours later as a chalky jet of indelible paint. But to the east, there are the mystery, the

promise, the light, the clouds of Mosquito Lagoon, timeless, endless, perpetual day of dreamlike, disembodied
lightness. Then a sunset, unlike any ever seen before,
heralds a sky straight out of the Arabian Nights, waiting
for the star of Bethlehem. When a rocket from the distant cape soars fierily into the black and dwindles to a
pinpoint in interstellar space, you try to visualize the
other worlds to be discovered by man across the ocean
of space. Canals on Mars, beaches on Jupiter, lakes on
Venus . . .

Chances are that none of them will equal the remoteness of Mosquito Lagoon.

A MERMAID

THE MERMAID figures largely in the lore of the sea. As far back as Odysseus, voyagers have brought home the fantastic story of the woman with a fish's tail, seafarers of all lands have kept the legend going. Some of them inevitably went too far, like the nineteenth-century story of a merman in Saalfeld, Germany, who came flapping down the village street at dead of night to look for a midwife to help his spouse in labor; on the whole, however, the fantasy of the woman with the fish's tail has produced sheer poetry. At the age of thirteen, when I was a cabin boy on board the hospital-church ship Rising Hope that followed the Dutch herring fleet as far north as the shores of Iceland, I saw my first mermaids. One misty morning, the bos'n called us boys to the deck in an urgent whisper. The bos'n was a big, uncouth man who somehow had retained an understanding of young boys; when my colleague Kris Muis and I stumbled breathlessly up the ladder from the fo'c'sle and emerged into the frosty stillness of the winter morning, the bos'n pointed overboard, black against the gray of the sky and the sea, and whispered, "There, on that ice floe . . . See them? Mermaids!"

We turned around, and peered, and our mouths fell open. On a water-slopped ice floe that looked as if it could do with a good scrub lay three creatures with bald heads, enormous moustaches and dissipated, red-rimmed, immeasurably stupid eyes, gaping at us the way we gaped at them. We felt a sharp disappointment, but the spell was thrown over us, the way it had been over countless predecessors, as soon as we discerned the creatures' most memorable feature: their breasts. They were not breasts likely to inspire rapture even in a delirious castaway's mind, but they were breasts, there was no doubt about it. It seemed as if, in the bos'n's hoary presence, our vision slowly changed. The creatures on their grubby slab turned into lithe, alluring sirens, their drunkard's eyes became golden, their whiskers wisps of blond hair blown, gossamerlike, across their lovely features by Zephyr. We were about to believe in mermaids for the rest of our lives when, suddenly, there came from behind us the angry sound of clapped hands; the creatures, startled, scrambled for the water and took a clumsy, degrading plunge. We turned round; there stood, like a bird of wrath, the thin, cape-cloaked silhouette of the ship's resident clergyman, Domine Zeilstra, a forbidding man full of self-righteousness, whose redeeming feature had been, so far, that he was seasick most of the time. "Thou shalt not lie to innocent children!" his harsh, cantankerous voice croaked in the shamefaced bos'n's poetic dawn. "Those creatures are fish!" His voice had that ring of ultimate truth which is the secret of prophets and impostors. The fact that he was wrong is immaterial; the creatures on the ice floe were certainly not fish but mammals; even so, he ruined our first mermaids for Kris Muis and me.

It took a lifetime before I came upon my next mermaid. I was exploring the waters around Flagler Beach on the east coast of Florida with Rival's tender when I entered a canal. It was so hallucinatingly Dutch, with its low banks, waving reeds and summer sky, that I almost expected Van Gogh's yellow drawbridge around the next bend. Suddenly there emerged, right in front of me, a huge, dark, breathy monster, bald-headed, bewhiskered, with two startled cow's eyes and a forehead two fingers high. Something in the way the monster gaped at me made it different from all other creatures that had, over the months, emerged close to my ship to take a swift look before vanishing like shadows. Alligators, turtles, snakes and otters had peered at me, but none of them like this: so sillily, so utterly flabbergasted. Whatever the monster was, it was a pacifist in a bellicose world. It seemed to be almost the size of the tender, yet it uttered, after a moment of paralysis, a wild, feminine cry of panic. Instead of vanishing like a shade, as the others had done, it made a kind of clumsy backward swan dive, with two shapeless flappers outstretched; in doing so, as it crashed obesely backward in its bath, it revealed the most staggering and unnerving pair of breasts it has ever been my nightmarish misfortune to set eyes on. She vanished, thrashing colossal shapeless limbs, and left a commotion of weeds, swirling mud and bursting bubbles. The bubbles went on rising for quite a while and I cut the engine and waited until they subsided before I dared venture on. I no longer expected Van Gogh's drawbridge.

The creature had been a manatee, but to help perpetuate the legend, let me record a true experience. In St. Andrew's Sound, Georgia, miles away from anywhere, one of the crew members of Rival was leaning over the rail, gazing at the dark blue water, when suddenly he saw a red-haired girl swimmer emerge at a few yards' distance from the ship. She looked at him for a moment, startled, then she dived again and vanished with a strong breast stroke of her pale slender arms. My friend grinned at her, because she was very pretty and obviously startled by the ship; only after she was gone and he turned round did he realize that the nearest land was miles away, that there was no boat in sight; no human swimmer could possibly be gamboling around in the strong current this far from shore. Yet there was no doubt in his mind, it had been a girl, with luxuriant red hair, in her early twenties.

I never questioned the truth of what he saw, for let it be quite clear that I consider Domine Zeilstra's interference with the sailor and his mermaid unpardonable.

MARINELAND

A DOZEN miles south of the ancient city of St. Augustine is Marineland Oceanarium, and it is a fabulous place. An inviting dock lures the passing yachtsman to its primly painted pilings, and there he is eagerly awaited by a fascinating old Irishman, the dockmaster, who charges eight cents a foot mooring charges plus one dollar fifty for electricity. Behind the dock, across the highway, lies a cluster of pink and blue buildings, gaily decked with bunting and flags, that harbor an unforgettable spectacle. Marineland, the Oceanarium, is astounding, not because of the sad, silent creatures locked up together in its main tank, a kind of submerged Bastille, but because of its trained porpoises.

All talk about the intelligence of porpoises will remain talk, like descriptions of the Grand Canyon, until the astounded spectator sits among a few hundred of his species on the small amphitheater, facing a pool with, in the background, painted on a whitewashed wall in gay lettering, MARINELAND'S EDUCATED PORPOISES. It is unbelievable at first, and later exhilarating, to see a band of porpoises perform all the tricks a dog would love to do but cannot because he is too stupid. There he is, Canis Domesticus, after fifty thousand years in man's company, but can he play baseball? Sing a hymn? Put out a fire? Ring a school bell? Get his books? Have his teeth brushed by the teacher while lolling, happily grunting,

on his side in the water? He can not; all he can do is
have himself towed on a surfboard, decked out in a degrading tutu, by a porpoise. There comes a moment at
the highlight of this performance that the whole thing—
Barney Murphy the dockmaster, Flippy and Splash the
porpoises, the dog in tutu on the surfboard and the naval
officer with the microphone commenting—adds up to a
reality that seems a glorious lie.

The full impact of the glimpse into the future you
have been granted while gaping at the leaping porpoises
in their pool penetrates to you only after you have
bought a book called *Window In the Sea*, which de-
scribes the method by which these giant clowns are
trained. The book, when read at night in your cabin, has
the supernatural effect of disengaging you from time
and place and granting you one single peep of Life on
this planet from God's point of view. The episode in the
book which does the trick concerns an earnest German
teacher, ex-circus trainer, and his pupil, a newly caught
porpoise, on the training lake, in the high fierce light of
noon. The teacher has been so eager to teach, the pupil
so eager to learn, that the porpoise has got the top of its
head burnt by the sun. So the teacher has put petroleum
jelly on its head, to ease the pain. There they are, floating in the gold and blue of God's compassion, a man in a
rowboat, a porpoise with jelly on its head alongside; the
man slowly, with quiet, insistent beat, teaches the porpoise a song; the porpoise, delighted, grunts in time. As
long as scenes like this are secretly enacted somewhere
on this planet, our future is safe. For if God makes me
watch them with tenderness and affection, why shouldn't
He do so Himself?

THE BEGINNING OF THE PAST

ST. AUGUSTINE is ancient, as America goes. A little town on a wide, swirling river, where flocks of shrimp boats chug past and hoot for the Bridge with the Lions to open, their bright yellow and orange nets billowing from their derricks in the wind. St. Augustine's fortress, gutted of its initial horrors, has been turned into a genteel and pleasant park, surrounded by a moat in which striped fish called sheepheads bask in the sun. There also are an old Spanish church with a delicate spire and one monstrous skyscraper, soaring above all, with on its top, in electric lights that never sleep, each new minute's time and temperature. On the waterfront a row of ancient horse-drawn carriages is waiting. They are open, with tasseled awnings; the Negro coachmen wear top hats, and the horses' ears are covered by little crocheted bonnets against the flies. The image of a Negro housewife crocheting a little bonnet with ears for her husband's horse and urging him to bring the other one in for the laundry stands guard over the town as an invisible sentinel, and her concept of time defeats the hysterical twitching of the minutes on top of the skyscraper.

There are narrow old streets in St. Augustine, with shops filled with water colors and artist's supplies, and bookstores ready to tell you everything about the history of the town; there are museums unequaled in weirdness, like Ripley's "Believe It or Not" Exhibition, which has a statue of Gautama Buddha for a doorman, or the Old Jail, filled with motionless mannequins languishing in chains while mice run up their trouser legs, or the Museum of Hobbies. Most enchanting of all, however, is Potter's Waxworks, advertised as "An International Educational Exhibit of Life-Size WAX-SCULPTURES, Meticulously Attired in Gorgeous Costumes of The Period In Which They Lived, From The Historic Past To The Present, Compiled by George L. Potter: Industrialist, Builder, Rancher with Creative Inspiration." Inside, the great men and women of history sit in tight rows along the walls, as if gathered on the balcony of a theater, watching an astounding performance. Two elderly ladies, schoolteachers, take turns guiding groups along the ranks of the great; to hear a literal quotation of what Henry the Eighth said to Anne Boleyn in a broad Dixie drawl is an enchanting experience. To listen to the charming lady, as she guides you kindly but without nonsense along the flower bed of history, is like reading a new translation of the Bible. Characters you have known for a lifetime as demigods and inhuman statues suddenly turn into neighbors; after St. Augustine, I will never think of Martin Luther again without hearing him say to those about to excommunicate him, "Heck, I'd love to oblige you-all, but I jus' cain't."

If the Negro housewife crocheting her bonnet is the guardian of St. Augustine, then the lady guides in Potter's Waxworks are the gardeners of its kind and cheerful soul.

THE SHADOW LINE

CROSSING the border from Georgia into Florida by car, the motorist will find huge billboards welcoming him to the Sunshine State. There is a "Welcome Station," where free orange juice is handed out to the pilgrims who finally made it to the promised land; it is the last thing they will get for nothing until, some weeks later, tanned and wiser, they will notice that there is no "Good-by Station" on the border, only a sign saying YOU ARE NOW LEAVING THE SUNSHINE STATE.

This border is entirely arbitrary. It has nothing to do with nature's truth, for the true border line between Florida and Georgia runs further to the south.

The moment you have crossed the mighty St. John's River on your way north, you will see that the landscape changes. No more palm forests, but romantic woods of live oak; the Spanish moss is invisible from afar, so the trees with their springlike young green evoke the image of a northern summer: flies buzzing against the window-pane, the smell of new-mown hay, white clouds sailing through a blue vacation sky. The first human settlement in this new land is the twin town of Fernandina, a live town to the south, a ghost town to the north: dead trawlers, dead factories, sagging docks; not a soul about in the streets, paneless windows swing in the breeze, a metal sign clatters against the wall of an empty drugstore, pelicans waddle clumsily on the weed-grown waterfront and at the dock, where once the fishing boats moored, roisterous and smoky and full of silver wriggling life, moss-grown sea-turtles come breathily peeping.

The most distinct shadow line between Florida and Georgia is an invisible one. It consists of a smell, a new nauseous stench that will haunt the traveler all along the Georgia coast: the stink of the paper factories is omnipresent, even in the remotest jungle of the colossal tidal forest that is the Georgia seaboard.

The first sound of the new land comes over the ship's radio, a local station from Brunswick. A bellowing bishop admonishes his listeners to mend their ways, stop sinning and mail their contribution now. Sister Ruby Johnson lectures rapturously about "Women, God's Gift to Men"; the spiraling crescendo of an uninhibited hymn seems to put an end to Freud's "Future of an Illusion," then a commercial advertises snuff, the time is announced as twenty minutes in front of seven o'clock, and the first light on the shore across the majestic Sound beckons in the evening mist.

To tie up to your first dock in Georgia is to step ashore in another world, a world of peace, pride and pleasant resignation. The Georgia drawl seems symptomatic of a slow, sleepy existence; wherever you stop to listen, strolling through a charming village full of huge empty hotels of yesteryear, you hear plans. Plans to change the village into a town, plans to build new roads, new bridges, plans for everybody to become different, go-getting people, real hustling Americans. You just catch them in the nick of time; tomorrow it will be changed, all of it, all of them, so let's relax until then, let *mañana* take care of itself. The park is full of tiny deer; the ship's dogs have the world's most dazzling beach all to themselves to cavort on; a doctor, who attends to minor injuries for nothing because he has no small change, keeps a cage full of twittering canaries in his consulting room and also his old mother, asleep on the consulting couch with a newspaper over her face.

Whatever people may say about the Deep South, it comes as a relief to any traveler from anywhere except, maybe, the land of Nod.

A MONUMENT

THE LITTLE town is all of Georgia: heavy trees with dark blue shadows, a one-room schoolhouse with a little lawn played bare, dusty roads, the smell of sea and honeysuckle; a boatyard with two elderly ladies behind roll-top desks who control a stock of fifty-three instrument panels that fit no modern engine, twenty-seven discontinued air horns and an icebox with Coca-Cola.

In front of the little schoolhouse stands a memorial, with flags, wreaths and guns of bronze, dedicated to the local boys who gave their lives for freedom in the Great World War, with, on it, one name. The soldier, remembered on this ornate tomb, was known to all, so though his body may not be there, his spirit is. His spirit pervades the village, the warm shadow of the trees in which he played, the little bare lawn where he watched the clumsy waddling of his first tortoise, the school bell that called him reluctantly to class and released him, yelling at the top of his lungs with the flock of his fellow prisoners: satchels swinging, yelling, yelling with the delirious delight of freedom.

Ceremonies in front of Triumphal Arches and Cenotaphs, resting on the remains of Unknown Soldiers, have no effect on the minds of the madmen who voice the hate slogans of the world. Maybe they should, at some time in their lives, tie up to the marina in this little town on the Inland Waterway, sit on the bench where old men draw hearts with their sticks in the sand between their feet, look at that monument with its one name, close their eyes and listen to the sound of the future: the count-down of children's voices, chanting a table of multiplication in the schoolhouse with the open windows, beyond the small lawn.

AN EVENING AT THE THEATER

THERE is, on the waterfront of another small town on the Inland Waterway, a pier with at its end a barn without walls: the local Playhouse. It is a theater in the round, open on three sides to the night, the frogs, the crickets, the smell of night-blooming jasmine and the probing searchlights of passing tugboats highlighting the show.

I saw my first theater in the round in Houston, Texas, and afterward asked one of the actors if he was not distracted by the presence of the audience all around him. He answered no, they weren't distracting at all, except for the flashing of their diamonds. Few diamonds are likely to flash in this open-air playhouse, as the audience is made up of loud-shirted summer visitors, little girls in evening gowns sucking peppermint sticks, and other lovers of the theater who disguise themselves behind whiskers and a beery breath and try to make themselves invisible by putting on old peaked caps in moments of self-consciousness.

I saw *Can-Can*, the Cole Porter musical, one warm, jasmine-scented night. The show was admirable in its courageous contest with the starry sky, the honking of bullfrogs in the reeds across the water, the whirring of crickets, the whizzing of fireflies, and the ominous, silent passage of a huge, ink-dark dredger, blacking out the stars as it was towed past. Under the circumstances, Thespis himself would have fought a losing battle for the attention of his audience; even so there were episodes that will remain forever in my memory: the song "We are Maidens Typical of Paris" sung by a chorus of young Mrs. Roosevelts in bonnets, a French judge with a crew-cut whose voice evoked a thousand graduates from West Point singing in the snow on the campus; a dance of gendarmes, so young that they had tried to suggest age by pillows under their uniforms, which resulted in the determined prancing of a ballet of mothers-to-be. Anything we professional dramatists and composers might ever contribute to the theater should be released only with the stern proviso that it shall *not* be exposed to the myriad twinkling eyes of the universe in the open-air theater on the Inland Waterway in Georgia. The crickets, the fireflies, the jasmine, the honking frogs, the tugboat and its searchlight—all combined to reduce the play to a shrilly lit little scene on a colossal simultaneous stage. Through the open walls poured in the turbulent memories of all adolescent summers, their promises, their dreams, their sins. If Shakespeare had been with us, he would have thrown it all into perspective; now all we mortals could do was to rejoice, inarticulately, in the glory of that midsummer's night and hope that it will be there forever, somewhere in the universe, where all time is recorded and transformed into the perpetual present of eternity.

THE SINS OF OUR FATHERS

SAVANNAH is a charming town, old without being quaint; its shaded squares are full of unself-conscious historical monuments. On Madison Square, for instance, there are General Sherman's headquarters, a house visited by Lee, a statue dedicated to a heroic sergeant of the War of Independence, an old gentleman leading a huge neuter cat on a leash to the grass of the Presbytery. From an open window across the square comes the quavering sound of a violin, playing a convalescent solo; the South, summer, Sunday.

The façades of the buildings on the waterfront, turned toward the city, are classic, stern and reassuring: THE PILOTS' ASSOCIATION, SHIPS' AGENTS, SAVANNAH ARTS CLUB. Opposite, antique shops with windows full of mementos of your youth: a china flask in the shape of a kneeling camel whose head comes off as a cork and whose tail is the handle, a white porcelain cat with gilded whiskers, asleep on a pillow with one eye open; a town where any-one from the Old World would feel at home. Let's go and have a look at the river.

The steps leading from the little square in front of the reassuring buildings lead down into the past. Suddenly, with the first chill of the dungeons, you are assailed by the horrendous specter of the sins of our fathers. The caves, the cobbles, the arched alleys to the waterfront, the rusty rings still cemented in the wall to which the chains of the freshly unloaded slaves were locked—the horror of what happened here still chills the spine of the idle stroller, caught off guard. The pain, the terror, the unimaginable suffering are still there, forever caught in those dungeons, and once they have assailed you, they will cling forever to your memory of the patrician colonial town above.

A quayside with rusty rails and weeds between the cobbles leads to the other Savannah: acres of dismal hovels, one of the worst "niggertowns" in the South. No paved roads, squalor, overcrowding. DOC JOHN, SPIRITUAL ADVISER: a huge orange-colored Negro in front of a fake Russian façade, complete with onion towers, that hides a ramshackle frame house, advising a cowed white-haired Negro couple. A hand painted on a sign outside a caravan: PALMIST—COME ON IN AND HEAR YOUR FUTURE. Then the warehouses, oil tanks and factories of the waterfront, and beyond those the jungle, two hundred miles of lonely forest through which the slaves once fled following the stars of the Drinking Gourd by night, hiding by day from our grandpappies.

For any visitor from the Old World, politely refraining from comment on the Negro Question, it would be a wholesome experience to visit Savannah. Go down those steps, visit the dungeons where the slaves were chained, and remember, you Dutch boys and English girls, whose grandpappies brought them here.

A RIVER

THE SAVANNAH RIVER, when approached from the sea, seems the fairest of rivers poisoned by the foulest of factories. The land breeze blankets Savannah's approaches with an evil-smelling smog, and ruins what can otherwise be one of the most magnificent welcomes any sailor ever got from the land.

Above the town of Savannah itself, the river comes into its own. It seems incredible, when standing on one of the high bridges and looking down on the delta of the mighty stream, that between that bridge and the town of Augusta stretch two hundred miles of river without a house, a dock, a landing, anything at all, except somewhere in the wilderness the ruins of a church built by Swiss settlers two hundred years ago, who were wiped out by the plague, and somewhere else the empty white circle of the terra incognita of our scientific age: an atomic plant, so secret that the whole region is left blank on the river chart. The chart of the river is for the use of the Army Corps of Engineers and mentions, as landmarks, "old oak tree," "cluster of palms" and "eagle's nest." Between Savannah and the sea moves a constant procession of ocean-going freighters, coasters, tankers, shrimp boats, lighters; above Savannah the only traffic is a towboat pushing one barge with a load of bricks to Augusta once a fortnight. The barge carries two huge head lamps up front, the towboat looks like an ocean-going tug with its yawning men coming out of screen doors and a cook turning over a bucket of peelings, slapping the bottom. These men have been under way for a week, and they would have seen more human beings ashore on the Amazon or the Congo.

The hundreds of miles of river above Savannah carry no message of dinosaur and giant fern, of alligator and otter, like its southern sisters; all it is is an endless river in which every bend is so much like the next one that the Army Corps of Engineers was forced to record such romantic landmarks as eagles' nests, hoping that their emissaries will make out as best they can.

The short stretch from Savannah to the sea may be poisoned by fumes and strewn with refuse, but it harbors the crown jewel of this mighty river. It is the ruins of an old fortress called Fort Jackson. Seen from the water, in its setting of empty sky, flat land and oily water like mother-of-pearl, it looks, in its basket of willows, like a scene on a Chinese teapot. Nearby stands a smug and well-kept beacon resplendent with fresh paint, a taunting contrast with the rotted old landing of the fortress, but once you have overcome your fear of snakes, tied up your dinghy to the pilings and climbed ashore, you will find a complete child's storybook waiting for you, open at its most delightful pages. For the old fortress, built as impregnable by those who make a profession of such undertakings, has been taken over by birds, treefrogs and a family of raccoons with a string of puppies who seem to be playing at pirates, with their black masks and their unconvincing attempts at menacing stances. To sit there and watch them is to lie on your elbows in the attic of your boyhood, to read once more in that book you remember hearing as a child: the story of the family of foxes, or the adventures of the three little seals in the Arctic, or *The Wind in the Willows* with Ratty, Mr. Mole, and Toad of Toad Hall. Behind you, freighters churn past at full speed, creating a surf in which the young raccoons play, and the Savannah River becomes unforgettable. For on its banks there is a monument, where the hatred, the lunacy, the pain and the sorrow of the Civil War have been dissolved into an atmosphere of innocence and peace.

LAND OF MAKE-BELIEVE

THE FATA morgana of the Straits of Messina is as nothing compared to the spell that the coastal swamps of the Carolinas throw over the mariner who ventures into their lonely wastes.

There is, for instance, East Ham Creek, a sheltered, pretty cove in the dusk, an ideal anchorage for the night. A pleasant farmhouse lies afar; a small yacht with a raking white mast is snugly hiding in the reeds; the remains of a small animal tragedy bob in the reeds on the other shore: the limp body of a white goose, graceful even now, submerged in death. It is a lovely place, peaceful, not spooky like some other anchorages in these sounds. Then why this restless tossing and turning after you have gone to bed? Why this waking up with alarm every other hour or so? Why is the ship so unquiet, the atmosphere so fraught with apprehension? It must be the night wind, hooting in the hollow turnbuckles of the shrouds. Or the physical exhaustion after a blustery day of sailing.

At last the sun rises like a red-hot iron ball out of the steaming jungle, and its fiery orange light reveals the truth: the pleasant farmhouse is a cluster of mangroves, whitewashed by cormorants, the raking mast of the little yacht is a dead birch tree, the bird in the reeds is a blob of foam, jellying in the wind. East Ham Creek is desolate, and haunted by a memory of evil.

There is, for instance, at the confluence of Cooper River and Calibogue Sound, on the tip of Daufuskee Island, any retired sailor's dream house: an old wooden frame house with a cupola on top which once served as a lighthouse, overlooking the rivers, the sky, the clouds, sheltered pleasantly from the prevailing wind by high trees with gently waving Spanish moss. Many bargees, fishermen and yachtsmen must have seen it from afar and written in their logs, *Lovely old lighthouse on Daufuskee Island—enquire*, envious of the lucky people living there now; prim white curtains, looped up with little bows, give the house a Victorian aspect and suggest horsehair chairs, an upright piano with *The Stephen Foster Song Book*, the brainless twittering of a parakeet at its mirrored double in a cage in the corner. It looks like a wonderful place to retire to at the end of a life spent on the water, to watch the ships passing from horizon to horizon through the most peaceful, luminous solitude any man might wish for as a setting to his last summing-up, before he sets sail for the great beyond.

Maybe one of them has been close enough to the reality of retirement to anchor off the channel and lower the dinghy to go and ask those people if the house was likely to be for sale in the near future. The aging sailor must have rowed briskly ashore, rehearsing his little speech, looking over his shoulder occasionally to see where he was going; then, suddenly, he must have glanced once more and kept on gazing, his motionless oars drawing two dotted lines of drops on the water. For the house is an empty ruin; the looped and tasseled curtains have been chalked on by some joker, long ago; the Spanish moss hangs in the trees like frayed old ropes, as if this ghostly courthouse, facing the void, had been the scene of a thousand forgotten lynchings. I don't know whether the aging sailor persevered and set foot ashore; if he did, he cannot have gone far. For if man has shied away from this promontory of doom, one species have found it to their liking and taken it over in teeming numbers: rattlesnakes.

The world of make-believe stops at Albemarle Sound, its last town has a harbor protected by jetties; even if it is still early in the day, too early to drop anchor, the passing mariner will be tempted by what he sees from afar: an attractive old city, one of the few cathedral towns in the United States, its spired tower rising from a cluster of old trees. Large colonial houses with colonnaded porches face the waterfront, oak and magnolia shade their lawns; it must be an Old World community of well-to-do Carolinians, a relic of the plantation era. The anchor is dropped; the crew rows ashore and finds that the town is inhabited almost exclusively by Negroes. The colonnaded houses have been split up into rabbit-warren apartments, the lawns are scuffed bare by children and digging dogs, and the cathedral turns out to be a grain silo. The only attraction for the passing mariner is the twelve-cent movies on Tuesday nights.

After visiting the town, I took the dinghy into the reeds of the opposite shore of the harbor, the ship's dog in the bow. We nosed up a narrow, winding creek and suddenly we found ourselves an ocean away, in the wilderness of the Westeinder Lake in North Holland, where I played as a boy, dreaming of Indians. Only a snake swimming across the creek reminded me that this was the New World and that, like all explorers who have been away from home too long, I had begun to notice similarities instead of differences.

A MUSEUM

CHARLESTON, South Carolina, is an exquisite town, still savoring its genteel glory of the early nineteenth century. Nowhere in America is the past so powerful; standing on the Battery, you can, by half-closing your eyes, almost see the seascape of the square-riggers riding at anchor. The signs on the façades of the shops in Queen and Meeting Streets are lettered in old-fashioned red and gilt, just as in Le Havre or Liverpool, and fill the sailor far from home with nostalgia.

Dusk in Charleston on a summer's night is unforgettable. The golden twilight tinges the white colonnades of the colonial mansions with pink and organdy; the air is heavy with the scent of magnolia and night-flowering tobacco; it is a favorite town for mockingbirds and when darkness is about to descend, the whole magnificent, scented flower basket turns into a music box that would have enraptured the Emperor in the legend of the Golden Nightingale.

Once the streetlights are lit, the town settles in an atmosphere of security, snugness and the dreamy adoration of a goddess called Crinoline; at dawn, old milkmen's carts rattle through the cobbled streets, reminding the dreamers awakening who they are: the keepers of a shrine, a priceless antique in this raucous world. The result is the atmosphere of a magnificent, haunted tomb. The living—an artist of *gourmandise* selling two hundred kinds of cheese with the delicacy of an archdeacon, a Greek restaurateur calling everyone "folkes," a convalescent old lady gingerly strolling in the shade of the magnolia trees on the arm of a nurse—seem to live under a cloud. Only by accident will the visitor from abroad stumble upon the heart of Charleston.

It is well hidden in a small room inside a dark museum with mock Grecian façade and two Sphinxes on its porch, given to the town by a donor whose bust seems ill at ease in the company of the two silent mythological spinsters. The art treasures inside are, at first glance, disappointing: rows above rows of badly painted, age-browned portraits of bonneted women and paunchy males, the kind of oils one finds in the better boarding-houses or on the walls of a stage-set if the hero of the play is a lord. As you wearily climb the granite staircase to the next floor, you notice a small door. Behind it, you will find the living heart of Charleston.

The walls of the small room are covered with miniatures, tiny oil portraits executed with painstaking naturalism, of the inhabitants of Charleston a century and a half ago. The burghers are pictured with an immediacy and a lack of flattery that makes them alarmingly real, more real than the people in the streets. There are shopkeepers, their pincushion eyes sparkling with greed; tight-lipped women watching the passers-by with venomous suspicion; obnoxious children squatting on tasseled pillows, looking at you as if you were a dish of tepid gruel; stony-faced and granite-hearted preachers; ponderous military with furrowed brows and blank stares; elder statesmen with foot-long eyebrows and hyena smiles—hundreds of small, magic mirrors showing the beholder the truth about man's nature, about himself.

In vividness and throbbing life, the miniatures match the descriptions of man in the early chapters of the Old Testament, where our true nature is revealed with total disregard for the niceties of Victorian convention, where Jews haggle with Arabs over plots for the graves of their wives, sons cheat blind fathers on their deathbeds, husbands swindle their spouses, wives sap the strength of their Samsons by night and absent-minded children dawdle at table, beset by dreams of fratricide.

The Charleston newspapers are full of plans to convert the city into a modern metropolis, replete with skyscrapers, windowless department stores and a university looking like a giant game of building blocks. But they who want to free Charleston of the spell of the past will have to blow up the Miniature Room in that museum first, otherwise all the new metropolis will ever be is a hot-dog stand at the entrance of this shrine of shameless revelation; the true rulers of Charleston will be inside.

For those who may be interested in the psychology of revenge: the miniatures are the work of a single man. Sometimes, the brush is mightier than the sword.

A MATTER OF FEET

APART from the terse bureaucratic jargon of *The U.S. Coast Pilot, Atlantic Coast, Section D*, the only guidebook to the Inland Waterway is Fessenden S. Blanchard's *A Cruising Guide to the Inland Waterway and Florida*. He is a highly reliable pilot for these waters, but he is a dramatic one. His excellent book abounds with ominous asides about sudden gales and treacherous squalls from which the author escaped by the skin of his teeth; apart from these interludes, which are likely to scare the wits out of the inexperienced, he shows a welcome and rare preference for the more rustic tie-ups and anchorages rather than the yachty marinas which are the same from Nantucket to Brownsville. Only in one instance did I find him wrong: in his description of the scenery between McClellanville and Mount Pleasant.

"Below McClellanville, the waterway follows a fairly straight and not particularly interesting course, chiefly through marshland, across and along innumerable creeks, rivers, sounds, bays and inlets for twenty-nine miles to the entrance channel to the next port, Mount Pleasant . . . one of the few parts of the Waterway we found monotonous."

I was amazed when I discovered that particular run to be among the most varied and fascinating of the whole trip. Near McClellanville, for instance, there are, behind the billowing reeds on the banks of the creek through which the waterway runs, the endless wastes of abandoned rice fields. Seen from the deck of Rival it was an enchanting and enchanted world, for the rice fields, abandoned by man, have been taken over by the birds. The ruins of slave hovels crouching among the waving wild rice had turned into rookeries, the mud of the shores was mottled by a thousand little feet, yet the individual birds seemed to be alone, as if they had found here a retreat from their society. As the ship slowly wound her way through the marshland, across and along the creeks, rivers, bays and sounds with their endless vistas, their sailing clouds, a feeling of space and freedom came over me, unequaled thus far. Blanchard must have felt very sour the day he passed here, I thought.

Only when I happened to cover the same stretch again with the Rival's tender, did I realize why Blanchard's opinion of that particular bit of the waterway had differed so much from mine. It was a matter of feet: when he came through here, his point of view was lower. Seen from the tender, the deck of which lay eight feet below Rival's, the marshes around McClellanville were all he said they were, because I was unable to look over the reeds.

Yet to me there was now a difference. Knowing what lay behind the high reeds on the muddy shore, I felt I shared a secret with the birds: behind those endless walls of unrelenting monotony lay the place to go to when everything else failed, a retreat from society, full of silver and sunlight, vast open spaces and hidden lakes, abounding with enchanting anchorages no man seemed to have seen. So I decided to keep silent about Fessenden's fallacy, hoping that all boats passing that way in the future would be low.

SHERWOOD FOREST, N.C.

CATTLERUN CREEK is a lovely anchorage in deep, muddy water, near a virgin forest that looks from afar like a painting by Ruysdael or Hobbema. The summer scenes by these Arcadian painters have an atmosphere of unreality about them, for those opulent oaks, those deep, shaded trysts of shrub and creeper never grew anywhere in Europe except in the imagination of the cooped-up men who painted these scenes to improve on the light green skies and the eternal clouds and the taciturn narcissicism of their stolid customers.

Here, at last, is what they saw in their minds' eyes: a summer wood of glorious opulence, full of honeysuckle and wild jasmine, filling the air with a scent of childhood. The moment you set foot ashore among the trees of the enchanted forest, they are all there: Robin Hood, Little John, Friar Tuck; this is Sherwood Forest as seen from a small iron bed in the top-floor nursery of an old house on a canal in Amsterdam, Holland, forty years ago. In the mud of the shore are the trails of Hobbema's deer; among Seegher's foliage shimmer the red and blue of Ruysdael's birds; and suddenly all the images of New

World landscapes retained in your memory seem to reveal themselves as the secret models of the Old World's
painters. The fantastic, agonized old trees that Rem-
brandt painted in his imaginary Israel grow on the banks
of the Atchafalaya River; the diagonal gray streaks that
Renoir substituted for foliage on the trees of the Forest
of Boulogne are a realistic rendering of the Spanish moss
that smothers Houston's oaks; Turner's visionary whorls
of light from which golden ships emerge, swaddled in
smoke, is a realistic picture of the fishing fleet leaving
Morehead City, North Carolina, at dawn. Even Ru-
bens' imaginary Moors are real and alive in the swamps
of the Carolinas: a small fishing village, deep in the tidal
forest, is peopled entirely with half-caste Negroes whose
skins are orange, whose eyes are blue and whose names
are Irish. To come upon these men on board shrimp
boats carrying names like Star of the Seas, Danny Boy
and Ike is to be met by Sindbad's crew: nothing on the
seven seas could be less real and more convincing. The
Arcadia the painters painted, so it turns out, the explorers
set out to find.

A CANAL

THE CANAL is one of the many dead-straight, well-kept ditches that link the sounds, the lagoons and the rivers of the Intracoastal Waterway. There is a smell of pine logs in the air that conjures up a vision of woodsmen brewing their coffee in the forest; the mushroom-shaped stumps of sawed-off cyprus trees, the hurricane gauges of the Army Corps of Engineers, the neat little milestones ashore all combine to make up a reassuring atmosphere of security and civilization, lessening the eerie unearthliness of this endless ditch running through nothing.

To realize the extent of that nothing I needed a breakdown of the fan belt of the engine of Rival's tender I was taking down this now-familiar road. I did not have a spare belt, the tender did not carry a dinghy, I was alone on board. There was no other solution but to drop the anchor, undress, tie my clothes in a bundle on top of my head and swim ashore.

Ten yards away from the banks of the well-kept, civilized canal, I might as well have roamed through the forest with the dinosaurs. There was not a landmark, not a trail in sight to reassure me that this planet was inhabited by the human species. I tied strips of my shirt to branches to find my way back, and stumbled, waded and crawled my way through the Mesozoic Age, carrying a broken fan belt No. BX114, which seemed as incongruous as an umbrella in heaven.

But soon man asserted himself in his full triumphant glory. When I crashed out of the thicket, after what seemed hours, I found myself facing a dilapidated trailer with in front of it, in a cane rocking chair, a stark-naked middle-aged male with glasses who turned out to be a Scottish scoutmaster.

It seemed, after a moment, quite logical to me, reared as I was in my infancy on the fairy tales of the Brothers Grimm, whose forests are peopled with dwarfs, wolves wearing bonnets, charcoal-burners trying to shake off their progeny by abandoning them in the woods and toddlers finding their way back by following a trail of bread crumbs they had surreptitiously dropped as Daddy led them astray. So I took the naked Scottish scoutmaster in my stride; his rolling R's among the palm trees, his broken-down car, the door of which had to be secured with a strap before we set out on a bouncing drive through the jungle to a neighboring gas station—it all seemed quite normal and sane. The owner of the gas station, seven miles away, shrugged his shoulders when shown the broken belt, and said, "I just took over this joint. There's a pile of belts over there in that corner. Just go ahead and help yourself." The scoutmaster helped me delve into the stack of belts and it was he who brought out, within minutes, the perfect match to mine. I paid the owner, was given thirty per cent discount because I was a friend, bucked back into the forest with my guide and drank a cup of black tea with him, chatting about Prestwick and Pitlochry.

The hike back through the forest, following the strips of my shirttails in the branches with the fan belt round my neck, the swim through the inky water back to the little tender whose gay Dutch flag lay mirrored in the black canal—it still seemed normal and sane until, a month later, I wanted to buy a second fan belt as a spare. A large garage on Long Island did not have one to match it; they wrote to the warehouse in New York, the warehouse wrote to the manufacturers, finally a letter came back saying they were sorry but this particular series had been out of circulation since 1934, and if there was still someone around using an engine that old, he had better get himself a new one.

I did not deign to reply. I sailed on without a spare fan belt, confidently awaiting my next landfall in the fairyland of the Brothers Grimm, otherwise known as the Intracoastal Waterway, Atlantic Section.

A SEASCAPE

WE MOORED in Morehead City on a wind-swept day in early summer. Most of the deep-sea fishermen of the region were in port because of the weather: huge white vessels, streaked with rust, with crow's-nests in their masts, surrounded by a flock of bumboats. We tied up to a jetty outside a restaurant on piles called "The Sanitary Fish Market"; the diners shook as we landed in the strong easterly wind. The town turned out to be wide open, swirling with dust; a railway line ran through the boulevard; rooming houses advertised FURNISHED APARTMENTS on signs swinging creakily in the wind; the North, at last, seemed near. The restaurant had a big notice board at the door, admonishing those about to enter that drunks would be thrown out. It seemed a sensible statement—let's keep the fish market sanitary. Morehead City seemed just a pleasant town in a well-sheltered bend of the waterway; no one on board was prepared for the miracle of the dawn the next morning.

We were woken up by the braying of raucous fog-horns, a sound of laughter, the clanking of iron. We all went out on deck to see what was going on and found

ourselves part of Turner's most glorious seascape. Day
was breaking in a glory of red, yellow, orange, green,
with surrealist clouds streaming out over the ocean from
the furnace of the rising sun. The Atlantic fishermen
were leaving; their silhouettes glided past in the triumphant light, gulls wheeled about them like bats. A black
ship came in against the tide of the white fleet; it was
manned by Negroes and looked like a piece of the night
returning. It drifted past us slowly, unforgettable; then
it lowered a boat full of Negro sailors in yellow oilskins
who rowed ashore through the flaming clouds mirrored
on the water. While the white ships dissolved in the
luminous vortex of Turner's sunrise, the dark ship
dropped its anchor, a huge rusty hook crashing into the
water with a splash and the thunderous rumble of the
chain rushing out through the hawsehole, spewing
brown dust. The rowboat hit the pilings of the Sanitary
Fish Market and its roisterous crew climbed ashore, full
of eager anticipation, oblivious of the inhospitable hour,
radiant with that irrepressible joy of coming home to
the safety of a port after a long, dark night of gales.

They rumbled down the wooden dock, past the Sanitary Fish Market, toward their mirage of a delighted,
convivial town. The moment they had vanished around
the corner, mean-eyed seagulls swooped down into their
empty boat and started gorging themselves on the tram-
pled silver that lay there, twitching, reflecting its last
dawn.

CHARON'S FERRYHOUSE

THE WORLD of the North Carolina swamps is a world of silence. To look at the banks of tangled dead trees and dark stumps standing far out in the inky water is to view the unimaginably distant past. This is how our coal looked when it was still vegetation, this is the image caught in the dark opal of the brontosaurus' eye. At night this silent world becomes haunted by surreptitious sounds: water drips everywhere, soft laughter snickers in the darkness, the feeble beam of your flashlight glistens in the dark caverns among the trees without revealing any life. Day breaks with low, dark rain clouds boiling behind the trees like the smoke of a forest fire; it seems to herald a different kind of day from the one we know.

The northern boundary of this eerie world is Albemarle Sound, and the last anchorage before the crossing is a narrow creek called the Little Alligator River. It may look different when entered from the north after the stormy waste of the Sound, but coming from the south, the Little Alligator River looks like the last landing man will ever see before joining the dead on the other shore.

As a child, listening among my classmates to my first lesson in mythology, I was fascinated by Charon, the boatman who ferried the shades across the river Styx. To a Dutch boy it seemed a familiar image seen in a dream: the misty river, its other bank shrouded in fog, a dock, the ferryman's house a dark shack on piles, surrounded by mythological trees, mirrored in the water. I pictured, in my childish mind's eye, the setting for man's last departure like a painting by Odilon Redon.

Decades went by; then, one evening, Rival entered the Little Alligator River, to anchor there for the night, and I felt the sudden, overpowering sensation of having been there before. I had, some time in the past, seen this river, those trees, that dock, that house. The house stood on a marshy point, on poles in the shallow water; I knew it must be a ferryman who lived there. The atmosphere was that of a frontier, and I realized that this was indeed the border of the South; as distinct a dividing line as the St. Johns River in Florida. North of us lay the summer of the old world: buttercups, daisies, chilly nights; south of us the reptilian smell of the swamps, the alligators, the vultures, the snakes. Maybe that was why the river gave me that feeling of familiarity; I had felt the same atmosphere in many frontier towns in the past. No one could possibly like the Little Alligator River for its own sake; it was too heavily burdened with expectations and apprehensions about what the morrow would bring.

As night fell around the dilapidated house and a mist began to shroud the other shore, I slowly realized that it could not possibly be a ferryhouse, for there was no road there. And then I sat on that school bench once more, listening to the teacher, savoring the pride of knowing Latin. The teacher slowly spoke two words, with lifted finger; I repeated them breathlessly with a feeling of giddy joy, a sudden, inarticulate realization of the abundance of the future, of life. "Repeat after me," the teacher said, "your first words of Latin . . ."

There it was, the ferryhouse, waiting for the voyager to whom it would reveal itself, with sudden ominousness, not as a station on the way to the future, but as the end of the road.

"Memento mori," the teacher said, and her pupil repeated it in a whisper, on the aft deck of his ship, in Little Alligator River, North Carolina.

6 The Atlantic
Seaboard, North

CONTENTS

THE HAGUE

THERE is, off the bustling harbor of Norfolk, well inside the town, a small, protected basin. Its pond-like surface mirrors the façades of old-fashioned houses shaded by trees; gentlemen in spats walk dogs on leashes to the neat lawn bordering the water. The well-to-do houses look as if they were occupied by notaries, dentists, retired judges and Mrs. Bartels, who discreetly lets rooms to students called "paying guests." On the other side of the cove is a marina with a dock too small for the ship; Rival swings sedately at her anchor in the gusts that ruffle the trees. Everyone on board is charmed by this setting of sheltered domesticity, its alternative being Chesapeake Bay in a thirty-five-mile north wind. Even so, we feel a little conspicuous on that pond, like the bandstand on a village square.

The pond is called "The Hague." Fifty years ago, this was farmland; a Dutchman bought it to turn it into a housing development. He called it "The Hague" after his home town and modeled it after its image; now the copy has become the original, for the section of the city which it resembles has been destroyed by aerial bombardment in World War II. The "Bezuidenhout Kwartier" in The Hague, Holland, is no more, but its reflection still trembles in the still water of a Norfolk pond. There are differences: Negroes hawk strawberries with a blues-like chant; a newspaper, floating in the water, carries the headline SEGREGATION OUR SACRED RIGHT SAYS GOVERNOR. But the similarities are more important: a dog barks at the call of a boy; a cat, its eyes closed in faint disdain, sits sunning itself on a window sill. Here, it seems, I tried out my first bicycle, glistening in the sunlight; here I strolled hand in hand at dusk under the scented boughs of the linden trees with my first great love, whose father imported marmalade from Scotland; my most poignant memory of her now is a stream of miniature sample jars that put me off marmalade for life. Here distraught women in torn nightgowns ran screaming from burning houses, while death and lunacy rained from the sky.

That part of the city of The Hague was razed to the ground; new, impersonal apartment houses have sprouted where once gentlemen in spats walked dogs on leashes to the little lawn on the water's edge. The town of Norfolk, Virginia, bustling, active, lives only in the future, oblivious of the fact that its secret backwater now mirrors a world that has vanished forever, with the great, the humble, the young, the old, the joys and the sorrows of yesterday.

ANNAPOLIS

ANNAPOLIS offers everything the visitor from the Old World has expected of Georgian America. The city is approached via Chesapeake Bay, one of the most beautiful Sounds in the world; the first inkling the sailor gets of what is in store for him is the sound of the bell buoys of Annapolis harbor, tolling like church bells in an English town on Sunday morning. His first view of the city will be the dome of the Naval Academy glinting in the distance behind the masts of anchored schooners. Most of the schooners are more than half a century old, white with gilded scrollwork and names like Caleb M. Jones and Miss Ruby Ford. A freak of legislation has kept these antique swans, called "bug-eyes," alive on Chesapeake Bay: motorized fishing is forbidden. So there they go, furling their old Bermuda sails as they chug up the channel to Annapolis harbor, pushed by dinghies with historic little engines that fill the air with a high-pitched puttering and an acrid stench.

The town of Annapolis itself would be a living museum and completely evocative of a gracious past, but for the common blight of most American towns: the telephone and power lines, strung indiscriminately along the ancient façades and across the narrow streets, in slumlike profusion. The houses of red brick and white paint are lovely and well preserved; the rolling lawns and ancient trees around the red-brick courthouse with its white-and-gold cupola and pillared porch give it an atmosphere of security, justice and dignity for all.

The heart of the town is the Naval Academy, and we were lucky to make our landfall just at graduation time. The evening streets were full of boys in spotless white uniforms leading girls in evening dresses like big butterflies of gauze to the graduation ball. There were hundreds of them; the next day as I watched the parade on the Academy grounds, I saw thousands. Thousands of identical youths, in identical uniforms, making identical movements; I realized that Annapolis is a town that feeds on youth. The dreams of the future admirals among the anonymous ranks of those thousands seemed more important to the life of the town than the leonine splendor of the old admirals who took the parade. As I strolled across the deserted Courthouse Hill after wandering away from the parade, I heard a distant gun boom out a salute of salvos and saw an old Negro, alone among the squirrels, stand stiffly to attention and salute.

The next day, I watched part of the unique spectacle of seventy-five weddings. Identical couples, with identical guards of honor crossing their swords above them for the photographers, followed one another in rapid succession on the steps of the church; then, two by two, they were driven off. The local youths of Annapolis seemed to have a thin time of it, what with those thousands of dazzling midshipmen skimming off the cream of the town's girlhood, so it is not surprising that there seem to be more than the usual number of leather jackets with snarling dragons on their backs, duck-tailed haircuts and tasseled motor bikes sporting flags with skull and crossbones.

At nightfall the tame white geese, begging and snattering domestically around Rival anchored in a backwater of the town, looked up at the sky. Overhead sounded the wild cry of their migrating brothers, echoed by the wooded banks of the river. It was a sound of adventure, freedom, youth, the sound of the dreams of Annapolis.

ARTIFICIAL ISLAND

HALFWAY up the inhospitable, murky waters of
Delaware Bay lies a flat, angular spill bank called Artificial Island. From it a breakwater juts out, making a
refuge for small ships caught by bad weather on this
treacherous sound. On the chart, the breakwater carries,
in small print, the warning "sunken ships."

Artificial Island is man-made and cannot be much
older than the First World War, yet it has the atmosphere
of an ancient churchyard on the outskirts of a sunken
village, for the breakwater is made up out of the hulls of
old wooden square-riggers, now rotted down to the
high waterline. Their broken ribs, jutting up at low tide,
look in the stormy twilight like the silhouettes of men
talking to one another from ship to ship; yet, after a
while, the melancholy that surrounds them is more
poignant than their eeriness.

After I had dropped anchor in their midst, having
cautiously sounded my way in, I experienced Rival as
being young and lithe. That night I lay awake a while,
listening to the wind and the distant throbbing of the
engines of the tankers on the river pushing their way to
sea. No cemetery ever gave me such a harrowing notion
of the shortness of life as this anchorage. This was the
end of the road for the proud ships who once were the
glory of the sea; now there they lay, wrecked and
broken, stripped of all pride, yet their awareness re-

mained. That was what gave Artificial Island its haunted atmosphere: they were aware.

Months later I paid a second visit to Artificial Island, with Rival's tender. I would not have put in there if the tide had not been stronger than I expected and held me back; I could just make it before nightfall. I was prepared for a haunted night like last time, the wind moaning dismally in the rigging, around me the silent envy of the wrecks in their motionless torment. After I had dropped anchor, I found an uncanny change had taken place: the ships' cemetery seemed no longer sad. The difference was the birds.

There were swarms of them ashore and more swarms overhead, spiraling black clouds of them; Artificial Island, that bleakest spot on that bleakest of American rivers, was a stopover for the giant flocks of migrating birds on the Atlantic Flyway. The wrecks, bared by the tide, gurgling softly with jets of water spurting through cracks in their planking, were now covered with a rippling blanket of millions of tiny birds that had made up the swarming clouds. And these were only the first to arrive; darkness had fallen when there sounded, close by, a loud, imperative honking, answered from the sky by a faraway reply. I looked through the porthole and saw on the water, close to the ship, the white shape of a pilot goose, calling in the flock. He guided them down as if he were manning a control tower, and in they came, immaculate V's of them, swooping down from the darkness, guided by his call; the rush of their landing filled the silence with a sound of breakers.

That night, I slept happily amidst the sleeping life around me, of which I was part. Toward sunrise I woke up with a start at a tremendous hissing sound. My first thought was that a dredger had anchored in the harbor overnight and that it was now blowing off steam, for that was exactly how it sounded. But when I looked out I realized that what sounded like hissing steam was the swishing of millions of little wings, as the small birds took off for the next leg of their voyage south. The moment they had cleared the sky, the pilot goose called the flock, and the white geese rose with an unforgettable sound of strength and joy as they soared into the sunrise, wheeled in the yellow sky, made up their immaculate formations and headed south.

The birds had done an impossible thing: they had turned the ships' cemetery of Delaware Bay into a place of hope and comfort, a place to remember in dark days ahead.

THE VENICE OF THE NEW WORLD

THERE are, to date, seven Venices in the United States, but not one of them even remotely resembles the Italian original. The nearest thing to Venice in the New World is a place called Ventnor City, a suburb of Atlantic City, New Jersey.

When you approach the town on the Inland Waterway, its skyscrapers determine the skyline to the east, while, to the west, there still are the mud flats of New Jersey. The approaches are wide and pleasant, though haunted by careening outboards driven by teen-agers; at the water's edge are small docks where elderly men in red hunting caps sit in rocking chairs, hopefully waiting to sell the old-fashioned motorboats that have become too fast for them and that now lie bobbing in the wash of the speed-hogs, with signs saying FOR SALE, OWNER LEAVING.

Atlantic City has a gay past; the traces are still there. "Lewisohn's Nasherei," a Ritz Hotel, large summer houses now rented as apartments. Old cars squeal round corners, most of them driven by women; a couple of unseasonal lovers lie shivering among the driftwood on the beach, "The world's finest." There is a Tea Shoppe called While-a-Wee and, in someone's front garden, an old-fashioned fire extinguisher complete with hose, brass nozzle and a card saying FOR SALE, PUTS OUT ALL FIRES, APPLY IN THE REAR.

At first sight, it seemed as if all fires had been put out for good in Atlantic City; then I heard of a strange migration of adolescents, twice a year, when droves upon droves of them descend on the town, the beach and the sand dunes in a lemminglike mating season. When I was there the only prisoners of love was the pair of goose-fleshed lovers in the rustling sands of the world's finest, but stories about the massive invasions of motorized Eros were the mainstay of barbershop conversationalists.

The unique and unforgettable part of the town is Ventnor City: hundreds of small wooden houses on piles line the canal, standing way out into the water; their verandas make up the roofs to boathouses. There the waterway is alive with snattering ducks, children in bright colored life jackets messing about in dinghies, balls bobbing on the water and toy sailboats with soggy sails wallowing in the wash. The houses, mile upon mile of them, look very gay, with colorful curtains, bold contrasting paint and husbands with their feet up on the railings of the verandas. Everyone waved as Rival passed; the children squealed like seagulls. When we stopped to wait for the bridge to open, a brace of pigeons swooped down on the foredeck with a flutter of wings and stayed there, cooing, tripping and nodding, until the dark shadow of the bridge as we passed frightened them and they took off again.

To those who feel at home on the water, Ventnor City, New Jersey, is probably the most congenial place in America.

WINTER

In summertime, the New Jersey coast is pleasant but undistinguishable from other pleasant seasides: Zandvoort, Brighton, Le Touquet. The backdrop may change, the atmosphere is identical: women in bathing suits sunning themselves on multicolored towels, children building sand castles, undulating blondes strolling the length of the beach in the company of a great Dane, followed by the somber stares of married males.

In the wintertime, however, there is no place quite like the New Jersey Waterway, as I found out when I passed there in Rival's tender during the month of November. There is, for instance, an anchorage called Little Egg Harbor: a flashing buoy in the frosty dusk, a shore line of white wooden houses, the sound of breakers behind the bar. Hunters in outboards return frozen from their shooting of the wild ducks, whose migrating millions give the southbound voyager the feeling that he is part of their great trek to the south, the sun, the summer. The night is cold, clear and windy; the next morning there is a great rush of wings as the first ducks pass overhead, and you weigh anchor and lumber after them, fattest of them all.

Then, the next night, a tie-up near another inlet: Billy's Pier. An ice-cold dock in an ice-cold village, where the little boat from Holland is welcomed by a bevy of ice-cold but delighted small boys. They look northern and wintry with their fur caps and mittens;

their questions make puffs in the frosty air. Seagulls wheel overhead; in the distance sound the volleys of the hunter's envy as they fire at the clouds of freedom rushing south. The little boys know no envy, they do not charge a pirate's ransom as ice-cold Billy does, whose day-trip business is closed for the winter; they knock on the deck of the tender at half past six in the icy dawn to ask when the boat is leaving and try to sell a photograph of it made with the smallest, coldest Brownie in the world.

When the boat leaves they are at school. I blow the horn in passing, because I know that the classroom will be still for a moment with upturned faces, listening to the farewell call of the only bird on the Atlantic Flyway that talked to them, and wore wooden shoes.

NEW YORK ARRIVAL—I

THE United States Intracoastal Waterway stretches unbroken from Boca Grande, Florida, to a little fishing town twenty-five miles south of New York called Manasquan. There the bargee, the tugboat skipper and the yachtsman have to take their chances and venture out into the open Atlantic and round Sandy Hook to enter New York Harbor. It is, to the uninitiated visitor, incomprehensible why twenty-five miles of open ocean separate the terminus of the magnificent Intracoastal Waterway from the largest city in the land, but there it is. Out you go, boys, and just you wait till the swell gets you. During her entire trip of three thousand miles, Rival took one nose dive and that was when she left Manasquan Inlet. She took over a ton of green water that startled the ship's dogs out of their wits, but once outside she smoothed her feathers and huffily paddled along the sandy shore into the fog that shrouded Sandy Hook and the entrance to New York Harbor.

To sail a fifty-year old Dutch canal barge into the largest harbor in the world is not a routine undertaking under any circumstances; to blunder into it, fat white goose honking her foghorn in answer to the deep-throated bellows of giant ocean liners, invisible but spine-chillingly close, makes for a memorable experience. There we were, hooting and listening, suspended in our own opaque little world; when finally some smallish vessel drifted out of the fog, we joined it to give us both a feeling of comfort, and found it was a red channel buoy. We lay at buoy No. 10 for hours, rolling in the swell, listening to the roars, the bells, the howling sirens of our sisters in the fog; finally it cleared sufficiently for us to crawl from buoy to buoy to Gravesend Bay, where we dropped anchor. We could not see New York; all we saw were isolated warehouses and docks.

Everyone on board kept saying, "This is New York, sure; Gravesend Bay is New York." But though geographically it might be, atmospherically it was not. We dropped anchor in the heart of Brooklyn; the natives who soon buzzed us in outboards until we rocked and rolled worse than at sea were predominantly Latin. It seemed another country altogether, totally foreign to New Jersey, and it had nothing to do, either, with the glittering Babylon of Manhattan. I took the ship's dogs ashore in the dinghy and landed at a place that called itself "The Gravesend Bay Yacht Club" but was known locally as "Nelly Bly." I was questioned by the locals in a gruff but friendly manner, and after a while the congenial atmosphere of the place got through to me. If Manhattan and its towers had not lured us on, this would have been a good place to stay, although the anchorage was exposed to the southwest and restless with the wash of the big liners that could be seen passing in the distance, once the fog had lifted: a stirring procession of the greatest ships in the world. The atmosphere of Brooklyn's waterfront was raucous and slummy but kind; the shore teemed with people, too many people too close together for refinement in human relations.

At dusk it began to rain; I watched the lights go on around Gravesend Bay. The sound of a pile-driving engine was the staccato accompaniment to the soft rustling of the rain. The crew of the ship Rival spent that evening on board, talking about the next day, and thus failed to profit at Nelly Bly's from the last comfort of human warmth and generosity before we landed on Manhattan's fabulous shores.

NEW YORK ARRIVAL—II

THE IMPACT of the skyline of Manhattan on those who see it rise for the first time from the morning mist as they sail up the Hudson River was demonstrated by the little ship's dog who had stowed away in New Orleans, escaped a tombstone in Clearwater and had romped about on deck and in the galley ever since. She was a gentle, tiny creature, apt to roll on her back at the slightest provocation, a gesture of abject surrender in very young puppies intended to demonstrate their tender age. She turned it into blackmail, for the next sign of surrender was to release control over the digestive functions; no one ever dared scold her, whatever her sins. This harmless, gay, affectionate little creature was asleep, as was her wont on chilly mornings, on the warm deck over the engine room. She woke up as we approached the Battery, stretched herself, yawned, sat up and looked, her ears cocked, at the world. At her first sight of the towers of Manhattan she froze, transfixed; then she started to tremble. She shivered uncontrollably, unable to take her eyes off the skyline of the city; the image of that little dog, trembling at her first glimpse of New York, will forever remain with me.

Hundreds of travelers from abroad have expressed their opinions on New York in print; I was in the city for too short a time to have any impressions but the most subjective ones. All I can say is that it's a great deal safer to sail a barge across New York Harbor than it is to cross the street. Some say that the cautiousness of the New York watermen is induced by the fear of being sued in case of an accident; to my mind there is more to it than that. The courtesy, good humor and impressive craftsmanship of the New York ferry captains express their awareness of their good fortune that they are taking a five-hundred-ton steel monster with three thousand passengers and two hundred and thirty cars across a mist-shrouded, swirling river and are not crossing Madison Avenue at Forty-Second Street on foot. Another opinion I can safely voice is that the Queen Mary, when tied up to her dock on the Hudson River among her fellow giants, seems small and that the floating Chinese pagodas that keep up communications with Staten Island make the Hudson and Manhattan look more mysterious and oriental than the Yangtze at Shanghai, when emerging from the early morning fog.

Otherwise, the atmosphere of the New York waterfront is much like any other big harbor. In the lee of its endless row of docks hovers a smell of vomit; contraceptives dot the water; in the little offices at the heads of the piers angry fat men in awning-striped caps converse over the telephone with enemies. The Seventy-Ninth Street Marina is a little world all to itself, guarded by attendants whose first names are sewn on their overalls. The harbor is full of permanent residents who live on board their boats; they let out their leashed bulldogs and poodles on the prim lawns of the park above, and understandably resented the invasion by two scruffy ships' dogs, lifting their legs at their mailboxes and cast-iron hitching posts. New York is so vast that it is split up into narrow, clannish villages of which the Seventy-Ninth Street Marina is one; above it there is the constant roar of the unrelenting traffic, and in the sky stream the four colossal black pennants of smoke from the power station, covering the city with soot.

Some have compared arriving in New York City to entering Aladdin's Cave; others have called it Babylon and seen visions of the towers of Manhattan gutted and empty, an eerie silence in the canyons of its streets, broken only by the mewing of gulls. All I can contribute to this repertoire is the little dog who had trembled as she set eyes on the city, yapping roisterously, wagging her tail in puppyish rejoicing when, after passing through the swirling vortex of Hell Gate, her world sailed into the blue serenity of Long Island Sound.

A GHOST IN
THE SUBWAY

WHEN I became a pupil of Amsterdam Naval
College, which took pride in its historic background, I
was, like the rest of the new boys, handed a book
written by a retired Merchant Navy captain. It contained advice for young sailors ashore in foreign parts; to
hand it to us at that moment was a stroke of genius. For
we were still a long way from foreign parts, doomed for
the next three years to confinement to the cavernous
barracks of the college and the concrete courtyard with
the concrete training ship, its yardarms and ratlines
scuffed bare by generations of cadets; a book about
how to behave in Hong Kong, Port Said and Valparaiso
made it all seem temporary and less bleak. One remark
from the old captain particularly struck my fancy: "If
you want to get to know a city, take the horse tram."
It was a piece of advice that I have followed ever since,
for though the horse tram had already vanished with
the author when I was given the book, it was obviously
not the horse that counted but the tram.

So, in New York City, I took the subway. It was just
after office hours; the train was full of commuters. There

were office girls; junior executives with narrow-brimmed straw hats; a few elderly people, gray with exhaustion. The atmosphere was one of resignation; no key to the mood of the city seemed evident. This subway train might be running underneath any major city of the world at this hour: the Tube in London, the Metro in Paris, the Underground in Moscow. Then a small communicating door at the far end opened jerkily, and in staggered a drunk.

He was an old man with a lumberjack's plaid cap, a short coat with moth-eaten fur collar and patched blue jeans. He came in with a rollicking shout of joy and slapped the nearest commuter on the shoulder, crying, "Ha ha!" He had reached that fleeting stage when a fifth of whisky has more effect on the human heart than two thousand years of Christianity. The junior executive whose shoulder he had slapped ignored him and he moved down among the benches, spreading cheer, good humor, snatches of song and, in the bends of the track, the hopping remnants of an Irish jig. His high spirits and passionate desire for communication with all his brothers on this earth were irresistible; then he came up to two adjoining benches where several young men, as identical as sparrows, sat talking. He pointed at one, indiscriminately, and said, "You remind me of me Oncle Henry, me boy," and he sang something tuneless but exuberant. Yet his ebullient joy seemed to be waning, and no wonder, because something was happening to him that I had never witnessed anywhere else on earth.

In any other subway in the world, had this man come in, people would have reacted with embarrassment or irritation, but they would have reacted. Women would have exchanged disapproving looks behind his back and men indulgent smiles; they might have tried to evade his insistent advances by ignoring him when addressed, but at some point they would have betrayed an awareness of his presence. Not so in this subway in New York City. It was not a tacit agreement, it was a natural mode of behavior; nobody gave any sign whatsoever that there was a drunk about in the carriage, dancing, singing, throwing his cap in the air, hanging on to the strap like a mischievous chimpanzee. They did not lock him out of their consciousness; he simply did not exist. The junior executives went on talking to one another across the aisle, even when the drunk, frightened by now, put himself between them. "Hey!" he called, his face swaying like a poppy amidst the straw hats. "Look at me! How are ye, me boys? Hey! Look at me!" But no one looked. The people behind the drunk's back exchanged not a glance, not the shimmer of a smile. They were not aware of his presence. He was invisible, inaudible, non-existent.

I saw a human being wake up in the other world, after death. The terror on the drunk's face when he was finally convinced that he was dead, a ghost in the subway, was unforgettable. He reeled out of the carriage in panic. He staggered through the narrow door into the next, a ghost trying to escape from hell.

The old captain's advice still held good. If you want to get to know a city, take the horse tram.

NANTUCKET

Fog is the keynote of these outlying islands; Nantucket is the last. When you approach the island from the mainland, there will come a moment when the fog clears, pale lemon sunlight slants down in a sheaf through the low cloud, and the golden cupola of Nantucket Church will sparkle with a flash like a lighthouse. After crossing the Styx-like waters of the sound shrouded in gray, Nantucket will emerge as a land of whitewashed houses, little boats bobbing at anchor in the bay, and a white church in a setting of green; a New England landscape painted by Grandma Moses.

Nantucket means different things to different people. It started out, as far as the white man is concerned, as a refuge for Quakers fleeing the bigotry of the early Puritans. Then it became a harbor of whalers and a home for lonely wives, whose husbands had little coops called widow's walks built for them on top of the opulent mansions where the ladies could stroll and gaze at the horizon. It is doubtful they ever did, but that was the way their husbands pictured them amidst the ice floes, the blubber and the stench of gigantic death in the Arctic. The dreams of the whalers, tossed in subhuman discomfort on the swell of the loneliest seas of the world, put their stamp on the town. Nothing in it has any roots in logic, all of it has been built to correspond to a dream. The houses the home-coming whalers built for their families are preposterous palaces of utterly impractical magnificence. One whaler had become so rich that he built a mansion for each of his children: five pillared palaces, white for his daughters, red for his sons. He must have dreamed them up in detail, while waiting for the cry, "Thar she blows," from the crow's-nest. It is fascinating to imagine his daughters living in these ridiculous mansions meant for New Orleans on a fogbound, tiny island, in a village with a feminine population of six hundred and a male population of ten. During their tea parties and their sewing parties, the ladies of Nantucket must have told themselves that the size of their places and the embarrassing expense were justified in view of the imminent return of their husbands; but most of them failed to return. Those who did built one of the town's most meaningful buildings: the Pacific Club. There the men who had finally come home sat shrouded in smoke, drinking, laughing, reminiscing; oil paintings of their ruddy features can still be seen there and their logs read.

But the spirits of the whalers are not there. If they are anywhere humanly conceivable, it must be on the widow's walks where they once pictured their wives gazing at the white horizon, shielding their eyes with a delicate hand. It never occurred to them that only a man can look at the sea for more than five minutes at a time; even with a houseful of servants a woman will always feel guilty.

THE HIDDEN FOREST

THE HIDDEN forest of Nantucket was first mentioned by the friends off whose dock Rival lay at anchor. They spoke about it in a tone of reverence as one of the wonders of the island, inaccessible to visitors or trippers, even to residents because it lay inside a big private estate. Only one man could possibly take us there, and they would contact him. He had come to the island every summer since he was a boy and was at present engaged in photographing the hidden forest during the various seasons. They rang him up and he was a little reticent; in the end, he agreed to take us there the next afternoon on condition that there would be no more than four people in the party and no kids. The idea of the hidden forest intrigued me. I pictured it as a haunt of elves and gnomes in a dell among the russet downs, a wood full of whispers and gossamer; and someone had mentioned ancient carvings which I assumed must go back to Indian times.

The next afternoon, our guide took us to the forest by station wagon. He was a charming, shy man with a peaked cap and a shapeless sweater, obviously knitted for him by someone he loved; his station wagon was old and battered and had a searchlight on its roof which, he explained, was meant to spot deer at night. As we made our way along well-worn tracks to the entrance of the hidden forest, I began to suspect that he was a poet bewitched by a vision we might be too pedestrian to share; he spoke of the secret wonderland awaiting us in words that evoked the dreamscapes of the old Arcadian painters. When finally we arrived at the gate, he hushed us and preceded us on tiptoe.

I was ready to follow him in his dream, and see the hidden forest through his eyes, but he was a better poet than I. He stalked the little wood with the rapture of boyhood; all I saw was a collection of trees and shrubs that might be unique on Nantucket because they grew in a valley sheltered from the gales but that were common anywhere else on this latitude. What the hidden forest amounted to for anyone from the mainland was a rather dowdy corner of any large city park. There were traces of picnics everywhere; the ancient carvings on an old oak tree, which I had visualized as the magic runes of forgotten tribes, were more recent. The first carving I spotted was a lopsided heart containing two initials, a plus sign and an exclamation point; then I noticed a whole line of words running along a branch of the tree. It ran MR. NIMBLE IS THE PISSIEST HEADMASTER IN THE WHOL . . . There it stopped because the branch was broken, probably by the weight of the scribe.

Maybe I should not have seen those carvings. Maybe if we had entered the hidden forest from the other side I might have shared the spell that bewitched our guide. As it was, all I could see, however hard I tried, were the same trees, the same shrubs, the same carvings, the same beer cans as in Central Park, New York. Obviously the hidden forest could only be seen by those who had fallen under the charm of that most elusive of goblins: the artist's rapture. The only secret flower blooming in the hidden forest was the poetry in our guide's soul, and to have seen that equaled the thrill of sighting a white whale.

TIGER LILIES

WHILE anchored in Nantucket Harbor, I read in the local newspaper, with interest and sympathy, an admonition to the tourists and the inhabitants of the island not to pick any more tiger lilies during their rambles on the moors. The small, delicate lily was typical of Nantucket, much sought after by the visitors, and their charm threatened to be their doom as the visitors pulled up the small bulbs when they picked the flowers; there were hardly any left.

I had to confess that I myself had been tempted to pick the engaging little flowers when I came across them as I walked the downs. Somehow this request to save them enhanced the feeling of security and civilization that made the island of Nantucket such a favorite place for summer residents. Every square yard of it must be known to hundreds of people, yet the downs were big enough to give one the illusion of solitude.

I forgot that the European idea of a walk across the downs is different from the American one. In the Old World, the walker sets out in sturdy shoes, woolen socks and in his haversack some powder to apply to blisters; he tramps across dunes, fields, moors and hills for miles; when he finally arrives limping at his always

too ambitious goal, he finds comfort in the knowledge
that it has been good for him. Not so in America. There
the walker gets out of his car, strolls in a circle, and gets
back into his car; so it may have been surprising but not
incomprehensible that during my third hike across the
downs I came upon a valley carpeted up to its brim with
millions of lilies.

It was a sight of such stunning magnificence that I
sat down where I was and gazed at them, lost in wonder.
The little delicate flowers, so dainty and fragile when
put in a vase three at a time, had turned that valley into a
cauldron of color, a crater of orange lava, rippling in
the wind. The valley had an atmosphere of utter solitude;
here, in the heart of the tamest, most parklike of American summer resorts, lay, aflame with a million flowers,
the image of Paradise before man was born.

Suddenly I saw another silhouette appear above the
crest of the hill across the valley. It was as if two lonely
wanderers, believing themselves unseen, had come to
drink at this water hole of beauty and suddenly found
themselves no longer alone. The silhouette and I remained motionless for a while, then, as if by mutual
agreement, we both turned away and retired the way
we had come. As I did so, I reflected that maybe I was
indeed turning into a crackpot as some people had fore-
seen, for delicacy may be a good thing but who on earth
in his right mind would want to spare the feelings of a
deer?

BETTY'S BLUNDER

ON ANOTHER of those walks across the deserted downs of Nantucket Island, I climbed what had seemed from afar to be its highest point. No roads led to it, it was miles from anywhere, it had about it a feeling of peace and remoteness that I had rarely experienced before. As I sat down to look at the view and let the serene atmosphere of the place soothe my troubled white man's soul, my eye fell on a jarring anachronism: a sign saying FOR SALE. At the foot of the sign lay a piece of rock, with, painted on it by an amateur, BETTY'S BLUNDER.

I instantly felt I knew Betty, and the man who had painted her name on that rock; I felt I knew what had happened here; it seemed as obvious as the sky, the wide horizon, the serenity of this highest hill on the outermost island of the United States. Betty, a housewife, had wandered over these downs alone, been caught under their timeless spell, and she had ended up on this hill where I now sat. She had gazed about her as I was gazing now, and the serenity of the place had soothed her troubled soul as it had soothed mine. She must have taken off her sensible walking shoes, rubbed her feet that were numb after this long unaccustomed hike, and all her vague fears, her worries, her doubts, the whole staggering burden that any young mother carries in this day and age had slipped away from her. In its place came a stillness, a hope, an inexpressible relief never before experienced, and she decided then and there with the resoluteness of love that she and her family should build a house there. She must have hurried down, suddenly afraid that someone else might stumble upon it; she must have gone to see a realtor in town, not waiting for her husband to come home from his New York office for the weekend. The realtor I could also quite well visualize, with his closed New England face, his calm dignity; he must have sold her the property in a hurry, for he too was conscious of the husband's imminent return.

And then, at last, he came off the noonday plane, together with thirty identical husbands, all with a narrow-brimmed straw hat with colorful band, all carrying a briefcase with homework from the office. She must have wanted him to come and see the surprise she had in store for him at once, but he changed first into his Bermuda shorts, striped T shirt, loafers, had lunch, snored on the sofa for an hour; then he let her take him there.

I don't know under what atmospheric conditions he finally arrived. Maybe it was foggy, the clammy, cold mist of the islands. In any case he must have been worn out when he finally stood, breathless and furious, on this pointless knoll without a road leading to it, without a hope of ever finding water, miles from the nearest powerline. He must have pointed out to her, with crushing patience, that to build the merest shack here would cost a fortune. And even if they finally managed to have something constructed on top of this mountain open to all winds and weather, did she suppose he was going to sleep a wink in New York, knowing her to be all alone with the kids in this godforsaken spot where she could be murdered, yes, and her mother with her, without anyone knowing about it until the next weekend?

He must have carried on for quite a while; the sensible arguments against building anything here were legion. But they were saddled with it now; the only thing they could do was to put up a sign, FOR SALE, hoping to God that some day another nut like her might roam about these downs and stumble upon this dilly the way she had done; and let's pray, honey, that she'll do so at the beginning of the week.

Betty must have looked up at him, mortified, and her decision was a foregone conclusion. He was the man she loved, and it was not the man that counted so much as the love. She apologized, crestfallen; she must have giggled when, mollified by the triumph of his masculinity, he put his arm round her shoulders as they walked back to the car.

I don't know when he came back to put up his sign. I hope the day was as luminescent as this one; I hope the glory of all that is good and creative and tolerant in the universe shone silently upon him, as it did on me this day. Then, as he gazed around him, maybe some doubt, some hint of what he was throwing away penetrated his soul. Maybe that was the reason why he erected on this hilltop his little monument of male triumph, asserting for eons to come how he had been right but had forgiven, as he painted on the lichen-covered boulder that had borne life for two hundred and seventy-five million years, BETTY'S BLUNDER.

A CEMETERY

THE OLD Quaker burial ground lies on the outskirts of the town of Nantucket. Its small, identical
stones with only a name and a date stand in neat rows,
like the crosses in the military cemeteries all over the
world. But if those crosses are reminders of man's seem-
ingly incurable folly, the headstones of the Quakers
on the isle of Nantucket are reminders of man's undying
hope.

Despite all romanticizing, no one can hide the fact
that the Puritans who settled New England were a narrow-minded, intolerant lot who brought to these shores,
together with their courage and their grim perseverance,
the seeds of the bigotry that still sprouts in the New
World like a weed. The Quakers of Nantucket were the
first to protest against the witch-hunts, the intolerance,
the self-righteousness which turned the teachings of
Christ upside down and man's elementary goodness inside out. The first white settler on Nantucket went
there, so he stated, "when he could no longer bear to

see a man treated as inferior because of the color of his skin."

The Quakers, best known to modern youth by the hat and the smile of the old glutton on Quaker Oats, were and are a remarkable sect because, all through their history, they have rarely succumbed to the infectious insanity called prejudice. The first white settler on Nantucket moved to the uninhabited island across thirty miles of open water only because he regarded Indians as human beings, his equals in the eye of God. William Penn, who started the colony since called Pennsylvania, kept a verbal treaty with the Indians alive and honored it for fifty years until the bigots got the upper hand at last and finished the "Holy Experiment" in a blood bath.

The isle of Nantucket is no longer an outpost of tolerance. The ideal the Quakers lived and died for, which is the ideal of all sane mankind, is now just as alive on the island as anywhere else. Yet, in some mysterious way, those little headstones of the Quakers overlooking the downs still pervade the atmosphere with a strange, elusive hope. To stand among them for a while, hat in hand, and feel the wind in your thinning hair and the sun on your aging brow, is an oddly comforting experience. It suddenly appears as if this feeling that something is wrong with the present world is a feeling shared by all aging males who mutely watch the sunset of their day. Suddenly the irreplaceable uniqueness of the individual seems to be stressed rather than effaced by these rows of identical headstones on the brink of the void of the ocean. Whereas the crosses in the military cemeteries of the French countryside seem to crush the individuality of the tragic youths buried beneath them, the identical headstones of the Quakers of Nantucket express the reverse, for they chose the uniformity of their tombstones themselves. Beneath each one of them rests the dust of an individual who, after a long and lonely battle within his soul, renounced his self-centered ruthlessness for brotherly love.

The Quaker cemetery on Nantucket seems a more valid monument to the United States of America than all statues, arches, capitols and other memorials put together. For theirs was more than the dream that the Constitution set for posterity as an unattainable goal. Theirs was the silence, and the love.

JAN DE HARTOG

was born in Haarlem, Holland, in 1914, son of a Dutch theologian. At the age of ten he ran away to sea and sailed with a fishing smack on the Zuider Zee. Since then his life has been divided between the sea and writing. His first great success in Holland was the novel Holland's Glory, *in 1940.*

During the war Mr. de Hartog escaped from occupied Holland and served in England. In the United States his name has become a familiar one through the success of his six previously published books, The Lost Sea, The Distant Shore, The Little Ark, A Sailor's Life, The Spiral Road *and* The Inspector, *and the great popularity of his plays,* The Fourposter *and* Skipper Next to God.

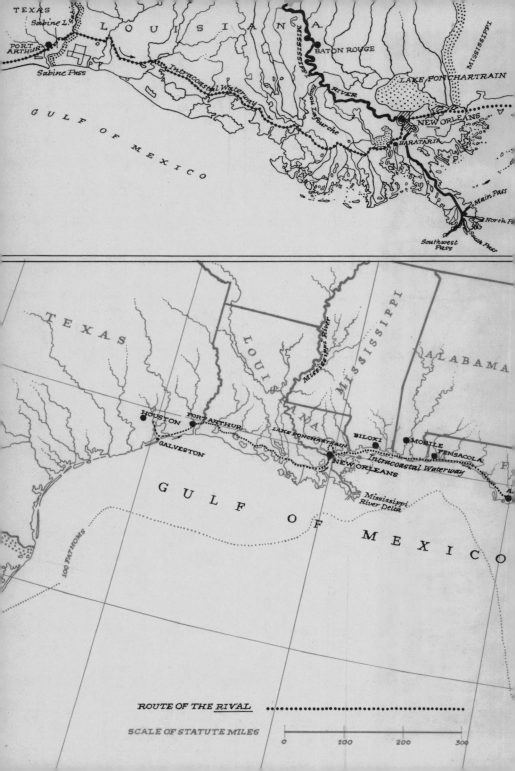

ROUTE OF THE RIVAL   ● ● ● ● ● ● ● ● ● ● ● ● ● ●

SCALE OF STATUTE MILES

0   100   200   300